The Real Business of

Other Books in the Gartner, Inc./ Harvard Business Press Series

The Real Business of  IT

How CIOs Create and
Communicate Business Value

Richard Hunter and
George Westerman

HARVARD BUSINESS PRESS

BOSTON, MASSACHUSETTS

Library of Congress Cataloging-in-Publication Data

Hunter, Richard, 1952–
    The real business of IT : how CIOs create and communicate business
  value / Richard Hunter and George Westerman.
      p.   cm.
    Includes bibliographical references and index.
    ISBN 978-1-4221-4761-0 (hardcover : alk. paper)
    1. Information technology—Management.   2. Management information
  systems.   I. Westerman, George, 1963–   II. Title.
  HD30.2.H864 2009
  658.4'038—dc22

                                                              2009019364

The paper used in this publication meets the requirements of the American
National Standard for Permanence of Paper for Publications and Documents
in Libraries and Archives Z39.48-1992.

From Richard

This book is dedicated to my brothers Mark Hunter and Jeffrey Sagalyn, both of whom I value in ways that are real but immeasurable.

From George

This book is dedicated to Clare and Henry Westerman, who are just beginning their journeys in the Real Business of Life. May they create and communicate great value in everything they do.

CONTENTS

ACKNOWLEDGMENTS

Anyone who has written a business book knows that it's a team effort. The team that contributed to this book includes a lot of people, and we are grateful to them all.

We are enormously indebted to the executives who contributed their time and insights to this book, including (in no particular order) Randy Spratt, John Hammergren, Gonpo Tsering, Dieter Schlosser, Ken Venner, Guido Sacchi, Sam Coursen, Doug Busch, Joe Antonellis, Kevin Vasconi, Rebecca Rhoads, Karl Wachs, Kumud Kalia, Marv Adams, Al-Noor Ramji, Larry Bonfante, Kamal Bherwani, Emily Ashworth, Jim Barrington, Larry Loh, Butch Leonardson, Trey Lewis, John Petrey, and Cara Schnaper. Without those contributions, there would be nothing to write about. We are especially grateful for the spirit of generosity that motivated their participation in these discussions—the explicit awareness among them that they have learned much from others and wish to give back as generously as they have received. Our conversations with these executives were inspiring, personally and professionally.

Richard's colleagues at Gartner have provided tremendous input and encouragement for this project, beginning with its genesis in a Gartner Executive Programs report in 2006 written by Richard with co-authors Tina Nunno and Robert Akerley. Richard is especially grateful to Mark McDonald, from whose lips he first heard the phrase "value traps"; Dave Aron, whose work on measuring value returned from initiatives is heavily referenced in this book; and Michael Smith, whose work on the Gartner Business Value Framework has significantly influenced Richard's thinking on where value appears and how it is measured. Richard wants also to acknowledge Louis Boyle, the creator of the run/grow/transform value model at Meta Group, and Audrey Apfel, Cassio Dreyfuss, Robert Handler, Bill Maurer, and Ken McGee, who contributed significantly to its development. Richard's current and former colleagues in executive programs research, including Barbara McNurlin, Andrew Rowsell-Jones, Mary Mesaglio, Heather Colella, Chuck Tucker, Patrick Meehan, Diane Berry, and Lily Mok, have offered invaluable constructive criticism, insight, and support for much of the research included in this book. Working with this team has been an extended highlight of Richard's professional life. Richard is indebted as well to his colleague Jim Hocker, to whom Richard uttered the phrase, "I can sum it up in four words: it's all about them" during a discussion between presentations at Gartner's Symposium/ITXpo conference in October 2006. In Nashville, we're told, if there are two people in the room when a song is written, they're considered cowriters. Following that principle, Jim gets half the credit (though not a similar share of royalties) for figuring out who it's all about.

Similarly, George's colleagues at MIT Sloan Center for Information Systems Research (CISR) have provided tremendous advice and attention, especially early in the research. Peter Weill was a collaborator in the early stages of the research, with IT as well as non-IT executives. Through numerous discussions and analysis sessions, Peter and George worked together to develop the concept of the virtuous cycle of IT value, as well as to dig deeper into the importance and meaning of effective business oversight of IT. Chuck Gibson read an early draft of this book and made valuable comments. Jeanne Ross, Stephanie Woerner, Jack Rockart, Nils Fonstad, and Anne Quaadgras provided useful research advice, and Chris Foglia, Tea Huot, and Erika Larson were always ready to help whenever they were needed. Special thanks are due to Mark McDonald of Gartner, who collaborated on CIO survey research related to IT capabilities and leadership and was a constant adviser on getting the messages right. Thanks also to Bud Mathaisel, Martin Curley, Malvina Nisman, and all our interviewees for sharing their ideas and insights on creating and communicating IT value, as well as to the many IT and business leaders who willingly shared ideas and examples during our presentations of these concepts. Finally, George is indebted to Cynthia Beath of the University of Texas for offering special insight at exactly the right time. When George mentioned to her in 2004 that he wanted to study CIO effectiveness, she suggested he start with the non-IT executives he knew through teaching. The perspective of non-IT executives has been fundamental to what we've learned since then, helping us understand that effective CIOs do more than manage their units well; they help the rest of the company play their parts in producing and overseeing value generation.

We are grateful in particular for the expert input, encouragement, and management skills of editors Heather Levy of Gartner and Brian Surette and Jacqueline Murphy of Harvard Business Press, as well as the advice of serial business book author Kent Lineback.

INTRODUCTION

The authors of this book have spent most of the past decade of our working lives studying and advising CIOs and other leaders in improving the management and business value of IT. In that time, one issue has dominated all others for most of these executives: how the CIO can show that the value returned for the enterprise's investment in IT exceeds the value invested.

It may amaze some readers that the value of something that has accounted for about half of all capital spending by businesses worldwide for years is in doubt. Indeed, if spending on IT is any indication, business leaders must know that IT has value. The problem is that they often don't know where to find the value or how to measure it—and in many cases their CIOs can't express the value in terms that make sense to anyone except another IT professional.

Many of the CIOs we have worked with are frustrated by their inability to communicate that they and their teams are the fundamental contributors to business performance they believe themselves to be. They feel permanently stuck outside the inner circle inhabited by the other members of the executive team. Most frustrating of all is these CIOs' conviction that they could improve business performance substantially—if only they had the chance.

Because this issue is of great and enduring—indeed, increasing—importance, several years ago we decided to focus our attention on particular CIOs: those who are acknowledged by their industry peers and colleagues as executives who deliver and communicate real value to the enterprises in which they work. At first it was our assumption that such CIOs exist and that their approaches to creating and communicating value would be potentially useful to others. Indeed, it is now our conviction that such CIOs are a substantial minority of all CIOs and that their numbers are growing as the practices and principles they live by—which we describe in this book—become more widely adopted in enterprises worldwide in every sector.

Most remarkable and inspiring are the strong similarities we discovered in the concepts and practices that have made these CIOs successful. The path to success for these CIOs is not only clear but also astonishingly common—not in the sense of ordinary but in the sense that it is shared. For this reason in particular, we think it imperative that it be shared even more widely, and that is why we have written this book.

The research behind this book is extensive and includes materials developed both independently and jointly by Gartner Executive Programs, Gartner Research, and MIT's Sloan School of Management Center for Information Systems Research (CISR), including the following:

- CxO surveys and interviews conducted by MIT's CISR, which have contributed heavily to research published by George Westerman and Peter Weill as early as 2005–2006 on the importance of effective business oversight of IT and the concept of the virtuous cycle of IT value, which we describe in chapter 4 of this book.

- The "CIO Agenda" surveys conducted annually since 2001 by Gartner Executive Programs, most recently under the leadership of Mark McDonald; these surveys of CIOs are the largest of their kind in the world (with a survey population of more than 1,500 in 2009) and offer a wealth of information about CIO priorities, budgets, capabilities, backgrounds, and aspirations. Analysis of survey results by Gartner and MIT CISR has contributed greatly to our understanding that effective governance, project delivery, and relationships are predicated on a foundation of effective IT operational delivery and that enterprise capabilities related to these factors are associated with different enterprise-level outcomes.

- In-depth interviews, beginning in 2005, with highly effective CIOs in companies that include McKesson, Freescale Semiconductor, CompuCredit, Broadcom, Gartner Inc., Boeing Employees Credit Union, R.L. Polk & Co., Sharp Healthcare, TIAA-CREF, DKSH, Intel, Analog Devices, Celanese, State Street Corporation, TRW, Solectron, BT, Novartis, JM Family, and others. Many of these interviews were supplemented by interviews with other members of the executive team, such as the COO and CEO, and by follow-up interviews in 2008 aimed at discovering where the practices and principles followed by these CIOs had taken them and their enterprises since our initial conversations.

- Other CISR and Gartner case studies we and our colleagues developed for research on related topics. Gartner executive programs researchers conduct almost 150 in-depth CIO interviews for research projects every year; CISR researchers are similarly productive. We benefit from many of these as direct participants in the interview process, reviewers of the material, or happy beneficiaries of the work of our colleagues.

- Our experiences teaching these concepts to hundreds of IT and non-IT executives through MIT CISR events and Gartner's CIO Academy, as well as one-to-one discussions with hundreds more.

We repeat that this research has led us to the strong conviction that there is a proven path to value for CIOs and their enterprises. In a word, this discovery is thrilling. It is a clear sign that the discipline of IT management, less than fifty years old as of this writing, is maturing in the way that matters most—as a proven contributor to enterprise performance. To say that we are at the beginning of a new era for IT and the professionals who work in that discipline is barely to hint at its importance. Because IT in the early twenty-first century is critical to the success of nearly every enterprise in every sector, public and private, everywhere in the world, the effects will ultimately enrich every employee and customer—in other words, all of us.

We are delighted to share this good news with our readers, and we look forward to hearing more stories in the future from CIOs who have followed this path to increase the success of their enterprises, their IT organizations, and themselves.

$$\left[\begin{array}{c} 1 \end{array}\right]$$

Take the Road to IT Value

ON APRIL FOOLS' Day, Intel's employee newsletter used to feature a farcical story whose joke was that it was obviously impossible. On April 1, 1998, the headline was "Intel IT Wins an Intel Achievement Award." Everyone in the enterprise laughed—except, of course, for the IT employees.[1]

Most IT organizations will never experience that kind of public embarrassment. But before you breathe a sigh of relief that it wasn't your IT team, ask yourself, Have any of your colleagues outside IT said anything like the following to you lately?

- "Why does IT cost so much?"

- "Plenty of companies succeed without spending a lot on IT."

- "We get results a lot faster in my department when we just do all the IT ourselves."

- "My son got our wireless network running at home in about fifteen minutes. Why do your people take so long?"

- "We could save a lot of money by outsourcing all our IT, and we'd get better service, too."

If you're an IT executive—the type of executive for whom we wrote this book—and you often hear comments like these, then you likely have the same kind of problem that Intel's IT team had in 1998. We might frame the situation as follows: managers throughout the business want value from IT, and they're pretty sure you're not delivering it.

And where you and the other leaders of the business are concerned, that's the end of any further discussion on the potential for IT-enabled value. You might like to think that IT could be an important strategic weapon for the business, and you might long to engage the executive team in conversations aimed at finding the strategic leverage points for IT—but you long in vain. Any attempt to start a discussion about the potential for IT to transform the business is met with stony silence.

If that's your situation, you're not alone. CIOs at many companies are frustrated by their inability to move the IT conversation to a higher level. For their part, business executives in many enterprises feel that their IT teams are not delivering enough value. As shown in table 1-1, these executives are baffled, frustrated, and even angered by their IT organizations.

No one can read that list of woes without knowing that something about IT has gone wrong in many businesses, whether in the value IT provides or in the way IT's value is communicated. Certainly any executive who agrees with any of the items on that list is suspicious of the IT organization's potential to improve enterprise performance. Such executives think of IT as a necessary evil, a

TABLE 1-1

Common attendee issues from MIT Sloan School of Management executive education course "IT for the Non-IT Executive"

- We're spending too much on IT.
- IT is a black hole.
- Projects fail to deliver.
- IT doesn't have a customer focus.
- We need to spend smarter.
- Should we outsource?
- Huge and unknown risks around IT.
- Lack of trust between IT and business.
- Our CIO speaks a foreign language.

cost to be diligently monitored and controlled, because the people supposedly in charge of the function are running a black hole that swallows up any resources that come near, emitting nothing in return.

The IT organization isn't the only one that suffers when IT value is in doubt. Because capable IT is as critical to business success in the twenty-first century as capable sales or marketing, the entire company suffers when the executive team doesn't see the value of IT. In effect, the enterprise gives up one of the most important potential sources of leverage it has.

The bad news and the good news

The bad news is that this is the IT executive's—meaning your— problem to solve. No matter how much any CIO might like to believe that it's the executive team's responsibility to learn how to appreciate the value of IT, the fact is that it's IT's responsibility to deliver and communicate that value. Period. Further, our research tells us that showing value is key to delivering more value—in particular, that effective business involvement in IT depends in large part on successful communication about the value IT delivers.

The good news is that because it's your problem, *you can solve it*. We know you can, because we have seen it done, over and over, at companies large and small, in every industry.

Our research on this subject includes surveys and discussions with IT executives and non-IT executives. It includes in-depth interviews with dozens of CIOs, many of whom are profiled in this book, and with several of the other C-level executives to whom those CIOs report. We have taken pains to base our research on the practices of successful CIOs, executives like Guido Sacchi of CompuCredit and Moneta Corporation, Ken Venner of Broadcom, Sam Coursen of Freescale Semiconductor, Doug Busch of Intel, Joe Antonellis of State Street Corporation, Marv Adams of Fidelity Investments, Rebecca Rhoads of Raytheon, Karl Wachs of Celanese, Al-Noor Ramji of BT, Kumud Kalia of DirectEnergy,

Larry Bonfante of the U.S. Tennis Association, Jim Barrington of Novartis, and Randy Spratt of McKesson. Unquestionably, these CIOs have delivered visible value to their enterprises, and sometimes have moved on to positions where they can deliver value more broadly.

Our goal is to help you achieve what these highly successful executives have achieved: recognition within and outside their companies that their IT organizations deliver real value—that they provide well-managed capabilities that are essential not only to running the enterprise at the best possible cost but also to supporting its continued and growing success.

Perhaps right now you can't do as these CIOs do. But it is our goal from this point on to show you how it is done. It is done, in fact, in a particular way and in a particular order, which we describe in the chapters that follow.

Nothing worth doing is exactly easy. The path to value described in this book takes work on everyone's part—yours, your team's, and your colleagues' throughout the business. The work is worthwhile because it pays off. It produces success for you, your staff, and your business—more value from IT, more recognition for the value IT produces, and more respect for you and your IT team as contributors to better outcomes for the business.

Start by thinking differently

The escape from IT's value quandary begins with something as simple and profound as a change of paradigm for the IT organization. We can sum up this paradigm change as rule number 1: *it's not about IT*. It's all about business outcomes and business performance, whether you're communicating IT's internal performance or IT's impact on business operations and financials.

Keeping that rule in mind—and acting on it—produces dramatic changes in the way the rest of the business thinks about IT value. No enterprise demonstrates the point more clearly than

Intel. After the embarrassing joke on April 1, 1998, Intel's IT leaders realized that they needed to change their ways. The story of their recovery is inspiring. CIO Louis Burns, who preceded Doug Busch in the role, embarked on a fundamental transformation of the IT function. The vision was that IT would be recognized as a key contributor to Intel's success, inside and outside the company. The two CIOs embarked on a series of initiatives that included consolidating the infrastructure, improving measurement, creating transparent governance mechanisms, and focusing continually on process improvement.

Every action was focused on delivering better value for the money invested—offering the right services at the right quality and the right price, and doing so in a way that made IT people easy to work with. Throughout the transformation, the CIOs made a point of communicating, inside and outside IT, exactly how IT's performance was changing in service quality and cost.

Their initiatives completely changed IT's service delivery, along with the rest of the company's perception of IT's performance and people. Total cost of ownership for PCs was reduced by more than 50 percent. Infrastructure unit costs and service quality improved significantly as measured by external benchmarks. By 2003, satisfaction with IT's performance had improved dramatically, with more than 80 percent of Intel employees surveyed rating the IT function as a strategic business partner (as opposed to a technology expert, provider, or vendor). These improvements were achieved while the IT budget was reduced both in absolute terms and as a percentage of revenue.[2]

Intel benefited greatly from its improved IT capabilities, and so did Intel's IT staff. CIO Doug Busch went on to establish the technology office in one of Intel's new business units. Other IT staff gained prominence both in the company and in the wider industry. And the IT unit was asked to take on the challenge of leading transformational programs for the whole company— a challenge that literally would have been laughable five years earlier.[3]

Successful IT leaders communicate value in a particular way and a particular order

The most striking thing we have discovered in our research is that successful CIOs, as a group, do remarkably similar things when it comes to achieving and communicating IT value. This is true regardless of industry, company size, or the portion of the company's revenue that is represented by its IT budget. It is true of public and private sector enterprises. It is true in good times and bad. It is simply how creating and communicating IT value is done.

We know that's a bold statement. Many IT organizations, like the businesses they serve, believe that their circumstances are unique. What works for others, they are sure, is far from certain to work for them. But we believe strongly in the power of the approach we describe in this book. It is not a magic spell guaranteed to win over even the most hardened executive Luddites, nor to immediately reverse a long history of distrust and suspicion between IT leaders and the other members of the executive team. It is the approach to creating and communicating IT value that has been proven in case after case and business after business. It fits with the way businesses build capability for managing IT and the way individuals build credibility as leaders.

It is something like redemption for IT, and all redemption— whether it comes via a twelve-step program, a religious conversion, or any other means—follows a common process. It starts by recognizing that you have hit bottom and that bottom is no place to be. You begin the change process by understanding how your thinking and habits have led to the problem and vowing to change. You acknowledge where you have harmed yourself or others. Then you start—first through baby steps and then through large leaps—to learn how to be the person you want to be and to reap the rewards of being that person.

Our research and experience show that IT organizations go through a very similar process. We can express the broad outlines of this approach—an approach that applies to you as an IT leader, and to the entire IT team—in a few lines. (See figure 1-1.)

- *Step 1: Change your thinking to avoid the value traps.*
  The road to (IT) hell is paved with good intentions. Avoid the *value traps:* practices that seem to be good ones but actually prevent IT from delivering and communicating value.

- *Step 2: Show that IT provides value for money.* As the "cheap information officer," you and your team demonstrate that the IT organization is providing the right services, at the right level of quality, at a competitive price.

- *Step 3: Show how IT improves business performance.* As the "chief improvement officer," you and your team help everyone make the connection between investment in IT and improved business performance.

- *Step 4: Show how you have value beyond IT.* As the "CIO-plus," you operate as a peer on the executive team, providing value beyond IT itself.

Successful CIOs don't skip steps, and they don't run them out of sequence. They don't try to demonstrate IT's potential power as a strategic weapon until they've shown that IT is beginning to

FIGURE 1-1

The path to IT value

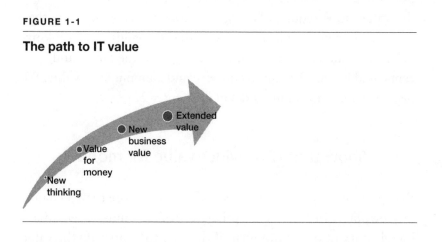

deliver good value for money. They avoid value traps, and they steadily increase the executive team's perception of, and involvement in, the value delivered by IT.

We examine all these steps in detail in later chapters. In this chapter, we introduce them briefly, starting with the value traps.

Avoid the value traps

Value traps are CIO practices and behaviors that at the time may seem correct, but that actually lead to trouble. They prevent IT from delivering value, and prevent the rest of the business from seeing the value delivered. Value traps are not about obvious failures, such as delivering unreliable service or being difficult to deal with. Value traps are more insidious. For example, saying that "the business is IT's customer, and the customer is always right" seems like a good idea when there is deep dissatisfaction with IT that stems from a long history of unreliable service. But over the long term, this value trap sets up the IT unit for failure, because customers are often wrong (especially about matters in which they are not expert), and calling colleagues "customers" puts a wedge between IT and the rest of the business.

The IT organization caught in a value trap is inwardly focused. That's a mistake, because in reality it's always all about business performance, and it's never just about IT. Overcoming the value traps requires IT organizations to recognize that they are in a changing environment, one that demands new thinking, behaviors, and competencies, beginning with the terms and concepts used by the IT team to conceive and communicate value. We discuss value traps in more detail in chapter 2.

Show that IT provides value for money

Recognition of the business value of IT takes more than a change in viewpoint. In many enterprises, executives must overcome a long history of disappointment if they are to appreciate the value generated by IT. Even when executives understand explicitly that IT creates value, they need to be shown that *their* IT organization is creating *specific* value for the business where it counts most. (Indeed, many of the CIOs we interviewed for this book were turnaround CIOs brought in to replace a CIO who couldn't—or in the most egregious cases, obstinately wouldn't—provide the specific performance that executive leaders considered to be critical to success. It's often easier for a new CIO to change perceptions than it is for the CIO who's perceived as poisoning the well.)

Successful CIOs begin to demonstrate and improve the value of IT by showing *value for money*. They make it clear— in word and deed—that the IT team earns its role as the company's preferred provider, every day. They report on IT's operational performance in terms of essential services and outcomes that are visible to the rest of the business. They link the cost of IT operations to the quality and volume of service. And they use unit costs and standard performance metrics to compare their services with those of other units or enterprises in an apples-to-apples way.

Many IT organizations provide their internal clients with gross statements of costs or chargebacks—in some cases, a single number that represents the aggregation of a myriad of line items. In such cases, the clients have no insight into the factors that affect their IT costs, no understanding of how to affect the totals, and no way to figure out whether the price is reasonable.

By contrast, successful CIOs make costs and performance transparent and comparable. They provide enough data to show where the costs are generated and in particular where changes in consumption of IT services can have an impact on overall spending. They show how much volume is being used, where organizations could use less, and where lower service levels in some areas might provide good-enough service at reduced cost. In other words, they give their clients information that the clients can use to control their own costs. And they always emphasize that IT is never merely a cost, even if there is a cost in using IT.

The most successful CIOs benchmark costs and performance and thereby invite comparison to peer organizations. There may be a reason that external benchmarking might not make sense for

"When you have operating failures, it's not that people want to make mistakes. You have to look at the process. Root cause analysis will tell you why errors occur. Metrics will tell you if you've improved."[4]

—Cara Schnaper, EVP, Technology & Operations, TIAA-CREF

a particular IT organization. But most IT teams profit from the exercise. In many cases, benchmarking shows that the IT organization's performance is competitive with what's available for a similar price on the open market. Where it's not, the CIO can make the point that performance gaps are now visible, and the IT leadership team will address them promptly. Either way, the CIO has a good story to tell, and the credibility of the IT team increases.

At this level, the "chief information officer" might be called the "cheap information officer." The services may not be exactly cheap; any service costs something, after all, and some cost more than others. Very high performance always costs plenty, no matter what it is or who provides it.[5] When the CIO successfully communicates value for money, the enterprise knows it is getting a competitive price for the right balance of quality (including, if relevant, internal user and external customer satisfaction) and performance. It also knows that the way to reduce IT cost is not simply to cut the IT budget but rather to adjust quality or consumption of IT services where excess quality or consumption doesn't improve business performance.

Communicating value for money is an essential starting point. Until value for money is confirmed, no other discussions of value are possible. Value for money can never be taken for granted; it must be confirmed every month or quarter, forever. But it is far from the endgame where IT value is concerned, and CIOs should be prepared to take the next step. If IT remains a value-for-money proposition forever, IT will be perceived only as a cost, albeit a well-managed one. The inability to perceive IT value in terms

"Reliability liberates you to talk about the business. It's not the endgame."[6]

—Butch Leonardson, CIO, Boeing Employees Credit Union

other than value for money can result in missed opportunities to leverage investment in IT for growth. So, after showing value for money, CIOs can and should take the next step.

We discuss the ways that CIOs can communicate value for money in chapter 3.

Show how IT improves business performance

Effective IT leaders not only manage well but also help their business counterparts play their roles in making good decisions about IT investments—decisions that produce operational and financial improvements in business performance.

By helping executives make sense of their needs, decide which will get investment, execute projects, and ensure that benefits are realized, IT organizations create a *virtuous cycle* that visibly maximizes the value of investments in IT. Mastering the four key tasks of the virtuous cycle improves the outcomes of each initiative, and creates capabilities that continuously increase learning and value with each new project. The CIO here might be called the "chief improvement officer."

In chapters 4 to 8, we show how CIOs and their business executive counterparts can implement the elements of the virtuous cycle. Chapters 4 and 5 discuss techniques that CIOs and their peers can use to identify opportunities for increasing value via improved use of information and automation. Then we show techniques for prioritizing those opportunities in chapter 6, tools to increase success in execution in chapter 7, and simple, effective ways to measure value delivered—the harvest—in chapter 8.

Show how you have value beyond IT

When CIOs focus on business performance and then deliver it, sooner or later they are perceived not merely as leaders of a technical organization but as business executives capable of contributing beyond their immediate organizational specialty. The change typically is gradual, but eventually quite significant. The first sign of this change for many CIOs is an invitation to join the CEO's staff meetings. The unmistakable confirmation occurs when you're asked to manage significant business initiatives outside the realm of IT.

CIOs often gain responsibilities beyond IT when they treat every initiative as a business initiative, demonstrate value for money, and measure the improvement in business performance resulting from every IT investment. Expanded responsibilities demonstrate that the business understands and appreciates the value that IT delivers—and that the CIO has become a business leader, and not only an expert in solving problems with technology. This recognition can go, and has gone, all the way to appointment of the CIO to a CEO position, as in the case of Guido Sacchi, former CIO of CompuCredit, who is profiled later in this book.

We discuss the CIO's personal value and the expression of this value as a member of the executive team—the "CIO-plus"—in chapter 9.

Build perception of IT value
from the bottom up

We have heard many CIOs lament that they never get the chance to engage the executive team in discussing IT's potential as a strategic weapon, or, when they do, no one listens. In most cases, those CIOs are trying to skip steps on the path. Typically, they haven't first built credibility by providing value for money, and so they haven't a hope of making the case for strategic value. Success results from building perception of value step-by-step, laying each tier of the foundation before proceeding to the next.

Bud Mathaisel, successful serial CIO at Solectron, Ford, and Disney, likens the path to IT value to Abraham Maslow's well-known hierarchy of needs model: "As I've thought about the best way to approach this, I've begun to think more and more about Maslow's hierarchy of needs. It starts with competence in delivering services reliably, economically, and at very high quality. It is the absolute essential to be even invited into meaningful dialogue about how you then build on that competence to do something very interesting with it. Because if you can't deliver in a reliable and efficient way, then there's always going to be a hedge on the part of the business partner or some suspicion, and therefore they won't go for it."[7]

In the end, the CIO who follows this path to value becomes a strategic peer of the other members of the executive team. Such CIOs do many of the same things other CIOs do, but they have much greater influence and impact. That influence and impact extend to the entire IT team. IT managers and staff, and the units they inhabit, gain direct benefits from moving up the path to value. They help their organizations achieve more value from their skills and disciplines, whether by improving efficiency, redesigning business processes, or helping business leaders (and even customers) gain more from their investments in technology.

It is no accident that most of the CIOs we interviewed for this book have taken on wider responsibilities within their businesses in the past few years. That's what happens when the CIO, like any other executive, is perceived as delivering business value; she gets the opportunity to deliver even more. CIOs following the path we have outlined have significantly improved the tone of discussions with the other members of the management team and have set the stage for further gains, often in as little as one or two years.

Guido Sacchi followed that path from the beginning for the IT team at financial services provider CompuCredit, where he started as CIO in late 2002.

When I got here, it was a turnaround situation for IT. What was in place couldn't sustain a new period of growth in the business. I was brought in to stabilize the situation and build a platform that would allow us to grow in a sustainable way.

I spent a lot of time with the business, and I tried to keep the discussion on business needs. "It's not about building infrastructure," I'd tell them. "It's about enabling growth. It's not about spending money; it's about getting new customers."

When I got here there were no metrics. It was mind-boggling to me—the company management was completely data driven, and we were producing metrics for everyone in the company but IT! I started reporting some metrics within about six months. I'm ashamed when I look back at the crudeness and paucity of the metrics, but it was an honest attempt to show the executive team that I was doing my best to be factual. Now, there's no difference in a budget discussion between me and another executive.

From the get-go I tried to focus in business terms: IT spend versus accounts, operating expenses versus revenue growth, how much we spend on running versus transforming the business. Just switching that focus, and communicating that to all IT—that our job is to make the agent productive, not just to keep the network up—made an amazing difference in a few months in terms of performance.[8]

Within a few years at CompuCredit Sacchi also took on the title of senior vice president of corporate strategy. As of this writing, he is the CEO of Moneta Corporation, which offers consumers and partners alternative payment choices for online transactions. The lessons he learned about the value of IT at CompuCredit have stood him, his former employer, and his new company well.

Like Sacchi, successful CIOs follow the entire path to showing IT value, from start to finish. They build on successes at every stage to get to the next. CIOs who don't do so encounter predictable problems.

- When IT delivers low value for money, the executive team either looks for a turnaround CIO or decides that IT is nothing but a utility—a cost to be reduced to the barest level necessary to keep the lights on, and not a penny more.

- When the CIO and his team fail to create transparent mechanisms for business oversight, IT is regarded with suspicion by the other members of the executive team, who have no way to know whether they're paying the right price for the right performance. They see the inevitable problems and difficulties that all IT units have, but they don't see the value as clearly.

- When the CIO and her team can't discuss the business in the same terms as the other members of the executive team, IT is doomed to be an outsider, an order taker— never a full participant in running the enterprise.

- When the CIO and his team can't connect IT investments to specific improvements in business performance, the executive team looks elsewhere for competitive advantage, ignoring the ways in which IT can be applied to differentiate the business.

Many CIOs will recognize themselves and their enterprises in one or more of these descriptions. If you do, you are not alone. But we trust that we have made it clear by now that this is by no means an inevitable fate for the executive in charge of IT.

Chapter 2 describes the starting point for the journey to IT value: changing the context and language used by the IT team members to conceive and describe the value they create.

Extended
value

New
business
value

Value
for
money

New
thinking

[2]

Avoid the Value Traps

When we are no longer able to change a situation,
we are challenged to change ourselves.

—Victor Frankl

VALUE TRAPS are beliefs and habits that seem to be good (or at least not to be bad) but actually lead to trouble. The organization stuck in a value trap is like the typical duffer trying to escape a sand trap on a golf course. The more he hacks away at the ball, the deeper he embeds it in the sand. Sometimes the only way out is to pick up the ball and move it to better terrain.

Value traps create barriers between IT and the rest of the organization, forcing conversations about IT into avenues that inherently reduce IT's value or place limits on how much IT can improve value. Value traps are often ingrained in the heads of IT leaders as well as business executives as basic underlying assumptions about the relationship between IT and the rest of the business.

As Albert Einstein said, insanity consists of doing the same thing over and over again and expecting different results. The behaviors that create value traps made sense in a different era,

TABLE 2-1

Value traps

The visibility traps

- We shouldn't have to talk about our performance; it speaks for itself.
- IT is a cost of doing business.
- IT managers deliver great technology for the enterprise.

The excuse traps

- Nothing is perfect (especially something as complex as IT).
- If you don't follow our rules, we can't guarantee it'll work.

The role traps

- "The business" is IT's customer.
- The customer is always right.

when there were different expectations for IT. Those behaviors no longer produce desirable results; now they are traps, not guides to success. Escaping the value traps requires breaking old habits and developing new ones that produce real and perceived value. In other words, it demands a new way of thinking and a new set of rules for IT management.

In this chapter, we discuss the habitual ways of thinking that pull the IT team into the jaws of the value traps (as shown in table 2-1). We describe how those habits destroy perceived value and limit the IT unit's ability to increase its actual value. And we show the changes you must make in each of these habits. We sum up with a discussion of how to think differently in order to visibly create and communicate IT value.

The visibility traps

Visibility traps are about the terms with which the IT team conceives and communicates the value it provides to the rest of the organization. Since all communication begins with an idea, it's appropriate to begin our discussion with the visibility traps.

"We shouldn't have to talk about our performance;
it speaks for itself"

In a recent conversation, one CIO told us that he doesn't like to blow his own horn, and that's why he doesn't report on the comparative quality and cost of the services he provides, even though he thinks the metrics tell a good story. Modesty is a classic virtue, of course. But the past and recent successes of P. T. Barnum, Richard Branson, and Donald Trump imply strongly that modesty is not a useful virtue in business.

Would the head of sales miss an opportunity to blow his own horn by neglecting to publicize the success of a new sales campaign to the rest of the company? For that matter, would the head of marketing fail to tell potential buyers about how the company's products stack up against the competition in price, features, and performance? Would the head of manufacturing fail to highlight improvements in the quality of manufactured goods or the reduction of unit costs?

We believe that executives, like everyone else, see what is brought to their attention. The costs associated with IT are brought to their attention every time they see a chargeback report or request a change in their services. Occasional failures are bound to be noticed, too. If IT doesn't make a point of bringing the value to their attention, it's much less likely to be seen and acknowledged.

Business executives shouldn't have to work to see the good side of IT performance. It should be made readily apparent, in language they can digest quickly and easily. Every one of the successful CIOs we have interviewed, without exception, reports frequently and regularly to the executive team on the value delivered by IT. CIOs who know that they provide good value need to make it clear to everyone. CIOs who are striving to deliver better value need to make it clear that they know what the problems are and are working hard to improve matters. Either way, spreading the news is the right thing to do, not least because it sends an important

"First, I hired really great, really smart people. I focused on enabling the [internal Broadcom] customer to do what they need to do. I put the IT people in with their customers. We defined the 80 percent of the routine stuff that IT people do as processes, so we could minimize the time and effort. And then we marketed it all like crazy, so people knew what we were doing and wanted to engage us."[1]

—Ken Venner, CIO, Broadcom

message about value to everyone in IT as well as the rest of the business.

Research at the MIT Center for Information Systems Research (CISR) with 153 non-IT executives shows that CIOs who are otherwise effective are seen as less effective if their business peers don't feel they have good oversight mechanisms.[2] If CIOs don't help non-IT executives understand what is happening in IT and how to make better IT decisions, those executives always feel at least a little anxious about IT performance. If CIOs don't blow their own horns, then business executives focus on what's most apparent, and that's usually the negative. Conversely, CIOs of struggling IT units find that they can improve their units' performance much more effectively if they put solid business oversight mechanisms in place. It's hard to hide the bad news, even if you don't make it clear. Enabling clear oversight helps everyone focus on what to improve first and provides easy ways to see each increment of improvement.

"IT is a cost of doing business"

A few years ago, one of us led a strategy workshop to assist an IT leadership team at a midsized financial services company. The workshop began with an exploration of how IT at this company added value. After an hour of discussion, the leadership team members were not able to find any way to describe their value-add except as running the company's IT at the lowest possible cost. They believed that they did this better than most, and they were baffled by their perception that the other members of the executive team didn't value IT's contribution very highly. But there should be no surprise that an IT team whose contributions are positioned solely in terms of low-cost IT operations is perceived as having little value.

We have no quarrel with the idea that it's important to run a tight ship, especially given that even frugal IT for a large business is not cheap. (A large manufacturer might be proud of an overall IT budget that equals about 1.5 percent of revenues, roughly 25 percent less than the average for manufacturers in general.[3] But 1.5 percent of General Electric's revenues as of this writing is close to $2.5 billion, and that is a nontrivial sum in anyone's terms.) In good times and bad, every business by necessity does a lot of things that are essential to staying in business but can't be tied to revenue, and these things should be done cost-effectively. Business activities such as audit and compliance with regulations (such as Sarbanes-Oxley), as well as many IT infrastructure services (such as dial tone and most information security), fall into that category—what many describe as *run-the-business* (or "lights on") activities.[4] The measure of value for these activities is *price for performance*—achieving the right level of quality (how compliant with Sarbanes-Oxley does your management want to be?) at the best possible price.

According to a 2007 MIT CISR survey, the average for-profit company spends 5.8 percent of revenue for IT, with 72 percent of this budget going for run-the-business activities.[5] Reducing costs for these kinds of activities (assuming that service quality is maintained at an acceptable level) is a valid goal for any organization. High-performing IT units can reduce the run-the-business expense to 50 percent, freeing up resources to improve the business. Indeed, doing so visibly is one of the key success factors in the IT organization's demonstration of value for money, which we discuss in chapter 3.

But if that's as far as it goes, the value contributed by the IT organization is seriously limited. Successful businesses do not just run. They *grow*, meaning that they increase profits from their existing markets and customer segments (or, in the case of a public sector organization, expand the scope, depth, or reach of their mission). Less frequently, they *transform*, meaning that they enter new markets with new value propositions aimed at new customer segments. If IT can't demonstrate its contributions to grow-the-business and transform-the-business initiatives, then IT is not a participant in the activities that make the business increasingly viable and successful.

To say that IT is only a cost of doing business is to position IT as a pure utility, like electricity—an undifferentiated commodity

---

The value of a database administrator outweighs the cost

A COLLEAGUE RECEIVED a recent inquiry asking for guidelines on how to estimate the relative value contributions of various IT functions, such as business analysis, database administration, and IT security. This is roughly like trying to quantify the relative value contributions of a car's engine and its transmission. The outcome delivered by the car—transportation in a certain style—absolutely depends on both. You can calculate the cost as the sum of individual contributions, but you can't calculate the value that way. (A marketer would note here that methodologies exist for defining the relative attractiveness of each of the car's features and functions to a buyer. It is possible that these methodologies might be applied to the level of service required for specific IT services, but we haven't seen it done.)

This is one reason successful IT organizations reframe the conversation. They report to the rest of the business in terms of services and the outcomes those services create, as opposed to the IT components that contribute to those services.

that contributes nothing to the enterprise's increasing success except for preserving its basic ability to do business. A CIO who allows or encourages IT to be considered in this light is essentially asking the business to dismiss IT's role in adding value. That is a prescription for failure, not only for IT but in many cases also for the business as a whole.

"IT managers deliver great technology for the enterprise"

The deep roots of most IT organizations lie in an environment in which IT personnel communicate mostly with each other in technical terms, and they judge success or failure by the performance of the machines they tend. These days, it is rare to encounter IT personnel who lack any understanding of the enterprise's business model and the ways IT contributes to its success. But for many IT organizations, a persistent orientation toward the performance of the machine—and not the business—remains, and this orientation makes it hard to communicate value to the rest of the business. Like any value trap, it is a behavior that no longer makes sense in a changed environment—an environment in which IT is expected not only to run the machines but also to contribute to dramatically improved enterprise performance.

The basic message of this chapter, indeed of this book, is simple: the right way to discuss IT performance and value is to focus on IT's contributions to business performance and business outcomes, and not on the performance of IT's machines.

"My CEO said to me, 'You've been succeeding in deploying the technology. But your job is to make sure the changes are deployed in the plants, and accepted and supported by management and employees.'"[6]

—Robert Proulx, CIO, Bombardier

"A lot of CIOs think they're customer focused, but they're going inside out. Look at the CIO dashboard—what do they show to the board? It should be things like new sales, the speed of closure, and how long it takes to open and close a product. Lots of IT organizations have metrics that say, 'We're 99.99 percent on uptime, we're fast.' The plumbing is wonderful, but nobody cares."[7]

—Butch Leonardson, CIO, Boeing Employees Credit Union

This is contrary to the practice of many (if not most) IT organizations, which is to report on their operations in machine-oriented terms such as network uptime. And we agree that the technicians who maintain IT's service capabilities need detailed information describing how the machines function so that they can tune and maintain them for maximum performance. But that is not about *value*; it is about *maintenance*. It is an inward view turned blindly outward. It is not what should be communicated to the *user*—the person who pays for the machine in the hope of a desirable outcome—and that is what we are concerned with here.

Some CIOs, and many other IT professionals, act as if they believe that their jobs are finished when the technology is installed. The problem is that from the point of view of every other executive, the job is finished only when the business achieves the outcomes it wants and has paid for. When IT teams deliver only technology, what they deliver is perceived in the same terms, and not as value.

One could argue that the success of a business change is the responsibility of business executives, and we are sympathetic to this point of view. But in an MIT CISR study, 110 non-IT executives put business process and organizational change on their lists of IT responsibilities, and not business responsibilities. Such executives recognize that they may ultimately need to pull the levers that make change happen, but they rely on their IT leaders to help them understand exactly what levers to pull and why.[8]

"When we have important meetings with institutional clients, the IT team goes along, because our clients know this is a technology business. We can drive business by being metrics driven around quality and efficiency in operations and technology. Our clients see it, and the front office sees it, too."[9]

—Cara Schnaper, EVP, Technology & Operations, TIAA-CREF

In later chapters we discuss in detail how CIOs can report on IT's performance more meaningfully. For now, we note that where IT operations are concerned, as with everything else, communicating value means remembering that it's all about the business, and not about IT. It's about what the business and its customers see and experience, and not the performance of the machines.

To help illustrate the difference between IT inputs and business outcomes, let's consider an analogy: the respective value provided by exercise and by an exercise machine.

What is the value of an exercise machine?

No informed person doubts the value of exercise. Even those who rarely exercise know that exercise promotes good health, vigor, good looks, and a host of other well-known and desirable benefits.

So that's the value of exercise. What is the value of an exercise *machine?*

If we measured that value in the same terms that many IT organizations measure their own performance, we would cite examples such as the number of hours per week that the machine is in use and the various grades of workout intensity that it supports. But such measures are all about the performance of the machine, and not the performance of the person using the machine, which is the real source of value.

Should we measure the machine's value as an asset? Certainly the machine can be bought and sold, depreciated and amortized, and so on. But in this sense the machine's value is not very specific to the needs of the person who bought it. As assets, an exercise machine and a television set might be roughly equivalent. But clearly, the value they deliver is not equivalent.

Ultimately the value of the machine must be measured in its effects on the person exercising—the *outcomes*—and not the machine's operations. Specifically, the value is measured in the machine's impact on the owner's performance—her ability to run faster and longer, to lift more weight, to wear sleeker and more stylish clothes.

But how is the value of the machine different from the value of the exercise that the machine enables? The answer is that the machine improves the effectiveness and efficiency of exercise in particular ways that matter. The owner can exercise on a certain schedule in a certain environment, with an emphasis on improving certain capabilities, at a certain cost. (When a particular kind of performance is critical, as in the case of an Olympic skier or professional bicycle racer, the machines used for exercise are refined indeed.) So the measure of value is that the machine improves performance more, and more efficiently, than do the available alternatives.

This metaphor can be extended to the language used to communicate the value of the machine. When someone decides to buy an exercise machine, he's not thinking about the treadmill belt going round and round; rather, he's thinking about how he's going to look in his new clothes at the big party in three months (see table 2-2). Certainly that's what the salesperson is selling.

But what is your IT team selling? In many businesses, the language used by IT professionals (and their peers throughout the business) to discuss business initiatives that include substantial investment in technology is skewed toward the machine—toward functions and features—and away from the desired business outcome. Many executive teams and CIOs—too many—talk about "an ERP project" or "Project SAP" when what they're really talking

TABLE 2-2

The value of an exercise machine is measured by its effects on the user

Exercise machine-centric metrics (value traps)	Exercise user-centric metrics
• Number of hours per week that machine is in use • Number of calories burned per user session • Muscle groups exercised	• Number of pounds lost since start of exercise program • Number of pounds to target weight • Maximum bench press weight • Time to run 100/200/500 meters • How cool I look since I started exercising

about is supply chain reconfiguration, or about "the CRM project" when they're really trying to improve their ability to find, win, and keep customers. It's the equivalent of calling an exercise program the "treadmill project."

The results of such misbranding are predictable and unpleasant. A 2004 survey by Gartner and Forbes.com found that the higher an executive was located on the organization chart, the likelier that executive was to hold IT responsible when a major project failed. Some 94 percent of the CEOs responding were likely to hold IT responsible for project failure.[10] Using language that implies that a project is all about IT contributes to those perceptions.

A focus on business outcomes begins with the language that is used to discuss business initiatives. In this sense, *no* project is an IT project. *No* project delivers technology. Every project is a business initiative focused on a business outcome that produces

---

"I pitched a million-dollar database upgrade to the COO, my boss, and he said, 'Nobody cares about the database. You have to pitch it in a way that everybody cares about it.' So we called the project the 'enterprise foundation project.' We told everybody, 'This is our foundation, and it has to be strong or the house won't be strong.'"[11]

—Trey Lewis, CIO, Campus Crusade for Christ

An IT presentation that is all business

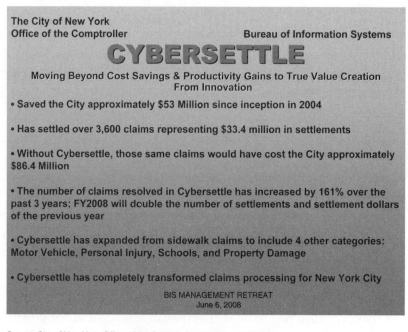

The City of New York
Office of the Comptroller   Bureau of Information Systems

CYBERSETTLE

Moving Beyond Cost Savings & Productivity Gains to True Value Creation From Innovation

• Saved the City approximately $53 Million since inception in 2004

• Has settled over 3,600 claims representing $33.4 million in settlements

• Without Cybersettle, those same claims would have cost the City approximately $86.4 Million

• The number of claims resolved in Cybersettle has increased by 161% over the past 3 years; FY2008 will double the number of settlements and settlement dollars of the previous year

• Cybersettle has expanded from sidewalk claims to include 4 other categories: Motor Vehicle, Personal Injury, Schools, and Property Damage

• Cybersettle has completely transformed claims processing for New York City

BIS MANAGEMENT RETREAT
June 6, 2008

Source: City of New York, Office of the Comptroller. Used by permission.

improved business performance—or else it has no place in an executive agenda.

Consider figure 2-1, taken directly from a presentation by Michael Bott, CIO of the New York City Office of the Comptroller, to his IT management team in June 2008. The only reference to technology in this chart is the word *Cyber* in the title (which refers

"No one ever brings me a proposal for IT per se. They bring an issue or opportunity, defined around the business, and IT is one of the pillars."[12]

—John Hammergren, chairman and CEO, McKesson

TABLE 2-3

Drive home the message that *all* initiatives are business initiatives

Don't say...	Say...
ERP solution	Manufacturing transformation
Network uptime	Point of sale uptime
Application development life cycle	Product development life cycle
Build IT Infrastructure	Support business growth
Install CRM	Get and keep customers

to the name of a system created by this IT team to automate settlement of claims for injuries involving New York City sidewalks). Everything else describes business outcomes, business value, and business growth. In short, the chart clearly conveys the message that this information technology organization is all business.

Table 2-3 lists a few examples of outcome-focused alternative language you can use to communicate about IT-supported initiatives with business executives in ways they can easily understand. These phrases are not mere marketing "spin"; they are more-accurate statements of the nature and purpose of the initiatives.

The excuse traps

Excuse traps are about how the IT team's execution and delivery are perceived by users.

"Nothing is perfect (especially something as complex as IT)"

It may seem obvious to say that the IT organization that wants to be taken seriously can't afford not to deliver reliably. But the legacy of many IT organizations includes a history of poor service and projects that failed entirely or were delivered over schedule and budget—and of executive management that tacitly has tolerated those failures by neglecting to hold anyone accountable.

In 1994, the Standish Group's landmark study of IT project management estimated that roughly 80 percent of all IT projects were partial or complete failures.[13] The situation has improved since then, but not everywhere. Recent Gartner research estimates that the failure rate for medium (over $350,000 budget) and large (over $1 million) IT-enabled projects is about 20 percent, with failure rates and the costliness of failures increasing as the size of projects increases.[14]) Such failures do not go unnoticed, we think. In Gartner's 2008 CIO Agenda Survey of 1,401 CIOs, 36 percent of respondents were classified as "at-risk," and 22 percent as "rebuilding," in terms of their relationships with the executive team.[15]

There are a number of reasons that IT organizations fail to deliver, including poorly managing IT processes or the business initiative pipeline, and mistaking IT priorities and risks for business priorities and risks. Perhaps the most important reason is simply that for most of the last third of the twentieth century, while the role, scope, and practice of IT were rapidly evolving— with all the false starts and mistakes that implies—many executives didn't understand technology or its capabilities and didn't know that they could demand something more and better. In other words, for many IT organizations, underdelivery is a long-standing habit for which they have never had to pay the piper.

But the fact is that they do pay. The IT team may think, "Nobody's perfect," but the rest of the business thinks, "Anyone who fails that often, and that big, can't be trusted." Worse still, executives no longer simply accept the idea that whatever they get from their IT organizations is all that can be expected. They see other companies using IT to achieve breakthrough performance; they know they can buy IT services from third parties. The IT organization that can't adjust its behavior to that changed perception is in a value trap that it must escape before any other discussion of value is possible. The new rule is that the IT team must never be seen as complacent about failing nor about accepting current performance as the best that can be expected.

Service management researchers have found that the way an organization recovers from failure is as important as the failure itself in shaping customer perceptions and loyalty.[16] When failures happen, IT managers must proactively show customers that they feel their pain and will do whatever it takes to minimize it. Then they should take visible steps to minimize such incidents in the future.

Perfection may not be possible, but excellence should be a given. Like managers in every other part of the enterprise, IT managers must work to continually improve IT's performance—and must be seen to do so. This involves improving value by reporting value, which we discuss beginning in chapter 3. It also involves mastering the virtuous cycle—opportunity assessment, transparent investment decisions, execution, and harvest—which we describe beginning in chapter 5.

"If you don't follow our rules, we can't guarantee it'll work"

Rules exist for a reason. Without rules, in IT and elsewhere, people create situations that increase risk. But when rules are rigidly enforced with little understanding or opportunity for exception, then the rules—and the rule makers—become obstructions.

Many IT professionals have something much like an engineering background: they started their careers as designers and builders of complex mechanisms, often in circumstances that required high reliability and predictability in the things they built. These professionals have an engineer's bias toward building things that work perfectly from the start. This bias is reinforced in many cases by experience, especially the kind of experience that follows the failure of a mission-critical piece of technology.

In contrast, business managers generally don't think like engineers. They tend to believe that "good enough" is a good start, and progress is usually more about making things better every day than about making things perfect on the first try. Indeed, one of the attractions of popular business methodologies like total quality management (TQM) and six sigma is their reliance on iterative, step-by-step approaches to improvement, which recognize and account for the fact that for most organizations it's a lot easier to evolve to perfection than to get everything right on the first try.

This difference between the engineering and the business management viewpoint helps explain the value trap that occurs when IT people rigidly enforces rules and standards without communicating why those rules exist. IT leaders know that it's difficult to deliver reliable, cost-effective service in a chaotic IT environment. Technology silos, masses of interface spaghetti code, aging technology, and unclear links to business processes create complexity that is hard to manage well, if at all. Costs and risks rise while reliability falls. Maintenance demands so many resources that there is little left for new initiatives.

Every good IT leader knows that the answer is to improve the foundation (as described in our book *IT Risk*): to evolve the existing complex mass of technologies to a smoothly functioning, well-designed technology platform.[17] But most enterprises can't do that in one step. The typical approach is to establish and enforce a technology architecture and a set of standards to guide the enterprise as its technology base gradually evolves in the right direction.

So far so good. But where IT sees necessary trade-offs that eventually will produce a manageable, efficient technology base, business leaders see hurdles. Every required business case is, to them, a bureaucratic exercise in hypocrisy. Every standard is another useless rule that makes IT's job easier by making theirs more difficult.

This is a complex value trap, not so much because it involves competing interests—ultimately, both parties have a strong interest in an efficient, smoothly functioning technology base, even if they don't think about it in the same terms—but because it involves trading off current, highly visible opportunity risks against future downside risks that are much less immediately specific and tangible. The problem is especially difficult because it is a universal human tendency to downplay the importance of future risks whose arrival and consequences are uncertain, and play up the importance of current, visible risks.

Solutions involve negotiations both formal and informal, including the transparent investment mechanisms that we discuss in chapter 6. Above all, the CIO must avoid becoming the

"The first thing I told my people was, 'Stop saying no.' They were seen as rigid and difficult; nobody wanted to work with them. Once we stopped saying no, the business's opinions of us changed. Then we could start making the case for why the rules were there in the first place."

—CIO of a high-tech firm

"C-I-No"—the permanent obstruction to business experimentation supported by technology.

As a wise man once said to us, "There are no technology issues. There are only people issues." This value trap is fundamentally about the people in the IT organization, their skills, their attitudes, and the ways they interact with the rest of the business. Recall the survey results shown earlier in table 1-1, which describes top attendee issues from MIT Sloan School of Management's executive education course "IT for the non-IT executive." Take another look at that list, and note that most of the issues reflect poor communication between IT and the rest of the business ("Our CIO speaks a foreign language" is a gut punch in that regard).

- We're spending too much on IT.

- IT is a black hole.

- Projects fail to deliver.

- IT doesn't have a customer focus.

- We need to spend smarter.

- Should we outsource?

- Huge and unknown risks around IT.

- Lack of trust between IT and business.

- Our CIO speaks a foreign language.

Preventing rules from becoming obstructions

SUPPOSE A TOP executive reads about the features of a handheld mobile device and immediately wants to equip every salesperson with one. When the CIO says, "We can't do that—there are security risks, it's not part of our architecture," and so on, what the executive hears is the word *no* surrounded by a lot of noise. IT will be branded as an obstacle, and the executive will start looking for ways to bypass the rules.

CIOs can achieve much the same outcome with less pain by making the case that the investment can be riskier than the executive originally thought. Just say, "Great idea! Let's see how we can make it work," and work with the executive to examine (1) where and how business performance will improve as a result of the new technology; (2) the costs—including all costs for purchase, training, and business process changes—to take advantage of the new technology; and (3) the risks, such as the potential business consequences of loss or misuse of the devices. At that point, the executive sponsor can decide whether the initiative is a go. IT can get to work, or not, as necessary.

At the least, the sponsoring executive will begin to understand important IT issues in her own language. She'll unconsciously begin to include those IT issues in her thinking about future projects. She'll also learn that the sales team must do as much or more than the IT team to realize improvements in business performance. Ideally, the IT team will gain a reputation for being the team that helps good decision making and makes great ideas work, as opposed to being the team that always says no.

Communication demands the right kind of people and skills, not machines, and it's no accident that the Gartner Executive Program's 2009 CIO Agenda survey found a dramatic difference in the relative priorities of the most-effective and less-effective CIOs where IT employees are concerned. As shown in figure 2-2, the most-effective CIOs put the highest priority of all CIOs on improving the quality of their people.

FIGURE 2-2

2009 CIO strategies by enterprise effectiveness

The most effective CIOs put a higher priority on the quality of their people

| | | Relative priority of strategy to CIO | | |
Strategy	Leaders	Challengers	Close followers	Late followers
Delivering projects that enable business growth	1	1	5	9
Linking business & IT strategies and plans	2	3	1	6
Reducing the cost of IT	3	2	2	2
Attracting, developing, and retaining IT personnel	4	7	12	11
Improving the quality of IS services	5	6	7	5
Expanding the use of information	6	11	9	15
Building business skills in the IT organization	7	12	10	13
Leading enterprise change initiatives	8	13	13	7
Implementing IT process improvements	9	4	4	6
Developing or managing a flexible infrastructure	10	8	11	10
Improving IT governance	11	5	3	1
Managing risk and exposure	12	14	14	12
Consolidating IT operations	13	9	8	8
Improving the business and IT relationship	14	10	6	3

Source: Gartner Executive Programs 2009 CIO Agenda Survey.

The role traps

Role traps are about relationships. IT professionals need to recognize the implications of the roles they have traditionally chosen to play in their organizations.

"'The business' is IT's customer"

Have you ever heard the head of sales, marketing, or manufacturing describe any other part of the business as his *customers?* Have you ever heard the head of sales, marketing, or manufacturing talk about "aligning" those functions with the business?

The only people in any enterprise who ever describe anyone except the people who buy the enterprise's products and services as "customers" are IT personnel. The only people in the enterprise who ever talk about "aligning with the business" are IT personnel. (Maybe the head of sales has talked about aligning her function with a new strategy or a new value proposition, or the head of manufacturing has talked about aligning with new key performance indicators—but aligning with the *business?*)

That view can't be good for IT. It is a legacy of the era in which the "data processing" organization was almost entirely populated with people who had very little day-to-day connection with the rest of the business. Those days are gone, but the mindset subtly persists, and it separates IT from the rest of the business in an unhealthy way.

What executives ultimately want from IT is not alignment, nor being treated like a customer. Executives want *outcomes*. Increased sales, increased margins, and increased market share are examples of the outcomes that executives want. If the IT team is talking about and helping to deliver those outcomes, then "alignment with the business" is a nonissue. But if alignment is the goal and the topic under discussion, then the IT team is in effect showing that it is not focused on the outcomes that matter.

Language is powerful. What we say can shape how we think—and it certainly shapes how others think about us. In this regard, calling the business a "customer" simply conveys the idea that IT is not part of the business. It establishes the IT organization as a vendor, and that has undesirable connotations. For a start, the interests of a vendor never coincide exactly with those of the customer, and when the chips are down a vendor can be expected to put its own interests above those of the customer. Vendors require supervision as well; a customer must always stay on top of a vendor to ensure that the vendor delivers what is asked. In the minds of many people, a vendor—even a reliable one—is not and never will be a colleague and peer.

The language has negative connotations for IT personnel too. Most importantly, it reinforces the unnecessary and undesirable distinction between IT and the rest of the business. It can lead IT people to focus more on funding and chargeback than on doing the right thing. Thinking of "the business" as a customer also leads to the idea that IT should do whatever the customer wants, a serious enough issue that we discuss it as a separate value trap in the next section.

Al-Noor Ramji of British Telecom puts it this way:

> I don't allow the use of "customer facing" unless those guys pay me real money. What was happening in our organization is that people used the word customer to imply colleagues. Now if you give me greenbacks, you're a customer. If you give me what I call blue dollars . . . it's just internal transfers of money. That's not real money. . . .
>
> So most of the spending decisions do come through me but . . . the budgets are still held by the business lines. . . . They cannot spend the money on IT without me. On the other hand, I cannot spend the money without them. It's very important that we have this partnership model, so neither side is seen as being able to do it on their own.[18]

IT leaders can and must show that they can deliver services as well and economically as any credible external vendor (or find someone else to do the job); that's the meaning of "value for money," the subject of our next chapter. But IT leaders need to go much further than that, and calling the rest of the business "customers" will, sooner or later, only get in the way.

We propose the "head of sales rule" as a simple test to ensure that the language CIOs and their teams use is appropriate: *If the head of sales wouldn't say it in those terms, neither should the CIO.*

"At the end of the day, I'm a business executive who's as committed to the top line and the bottom line as any other executive."[19]

—Guido Sacchi, CEO, Moneta Corporation (former CIO, CompuCredit)

The head-of-sales rule isn't infallible. As we discuss later in this book, there are good reasons that a CIO needs to talk about governance and the head of sales doesn't. But the rule works for most of the things that IT does, and it's a good gut check for the language CIOs use to discuss business.

"The customer is always right"

Thinking of the rest of the business as IT's customers and focusing on alignment with the business tend to lead IT to the ideas that the customer is always right and that the customer-focused thing to do is to respond immediately to any request. But in the absence of a larger design, delivering without question on every request is a value trap. Over time, setting up IT as an order taker produces the complicated, brittle, and expensive legacy environments that most mature enterprises have. It hurts the business's ability to deliver what's needed for the future. Even when demand for IT's services is apparently under control, rushing to deliver creates future demand that is sure to exceed supply.

These dangers, which are ultimately about agility, are illustrated vividly by what happened to high-tech manufacturer Tektronix in the 1990s. For years, the IT unit had delivered what the business wanted, on demand. Each new request patched the existing systems and connected them in an increasingly complex and undocumented spiderweb of interfaces. It became increasingly difficult and time-consuming for IT to deliver on the enterprise's demands both great and small, and of course IT took the blame for this visible deterioration in responsiveness. The situation came to a head when management found out that it could not divest a division because its systems were too densely intertwined with the systems of other divisions. That got everyone's attention. The management team had to invest heavily to improve the enterprise's IT systems and governance processes so that it could generate the kind of value it needed from its IT investments.[20]

As CIO Al-Noor Ramji of British Telecom says, "If they're not spending money wisely, we should have a row about it."[21] When a business executive describes how business performance must change, he almost certainly knows what he's talking about; but when it comes to how systems and business processes should be changed to achieve the goal, he may well be wrong. By helping the business clarify the desired outcomes and providing meaningful input on technology-supported business process change, IT leaders can help the customer get what he really needs, and not only what he's asking for. We discuss how in chapters 5 and 6.

We caution that pushing back is not the same as insisting that everyone follow IT's rules. Balancing the two is a complex process that depends on the situation and your relationship with the person requesting your resources. Pushing back effectively starts with a foundation of credibility that comes from effective delivery.

Change the behaviors that create value traps

Table 2-4 summarizes our discussion of value traps. It shows the old beliefs, the new realities for IT that make the old ones dangerously obsolete, and the changes you must make to escape each value trap.

The fundamental error in all value traps is to put the IT machine, as opposed to the business outcome, at the center of the discussion. In the end, it's all about the performance of the business, and not the performance of the machine.

Next, we look at the ways successful CIOs take the second step on the path to visible IT value: establishing the IT organization in fact and reputation as a reliable, cost-effective service provider that imparts value for money.

"We create a game plan for each process—supply chain, manufacturing, and so on—and get that locked in with the owner of the process. So instead of running around doing a thousand little fixes, which users can easily make you do—and none of the fixes have ROI—we can focus on the big steps."[22]

—Sam Coursen, CIO, Freescale Semiconductor

TABLE 2-4

Value traps and new realities

IT's old belief	The new reality	What must change
We shouldn't have to talk about our performance; it speaks for itself.	People see only what affects them most, and that's usually the problems.	Constantly measure and publicize performance. Express IT's performance in terms that connect to the performance of the business.
IT is a cost of doing business.	If IT is only a cost, then it's something to be constantly reduced.	Never convey cost without conveying value and performance.
IT managers deliver great technology for the enterprise	Technology is not an outcome. It sets up CIOs to get credit for cost and trouble, but not for value.	Because IT's value comes from changing the way the business works, IT leaders must help deliver business change. At a minimum, help business leaders understand what levers they need to pull.
Nothing is perfect (especially anything as complex as IT).	If IT fails when the chips are down, IT can't be trusted. If we don't discuss how much failure is too much, then it's always too much. And if we don't take a customer focus on recovery then every failure creates animosity.	IT's performance must be continuously, visibly improved, including by measuring—and learning from—failures. And when addressing failures, IT should practice customer focused "service recovery."
If you don't follow our rules, we can't guarantee it'll work.	Focusing on rules instead of reasons doesn't make IT look helpful. If business leaders can't see the rationale for the rules, then IT is an obstruction.	Everyone understands why the rules are there. IT has a smooth method to consider requests for exceptions and a proactive way to change standards when needed.
"The business" is IT's customer.	IT should be a peer and not a vendor.	Use the head-of-sales rule— don't position IT as a special case and something apart from everything else.
The customer is always right.	Business executives need business change, not specific technologies. And they don't often want to pay for important capabilities that don't have direct payoff to their units' plans.	Help the business focus on what it needs to deliver improved performance, not just what it asks for. Make the case for enterprise funding of foundational infrastructure and capability investments that no specific business unit would request on its own.

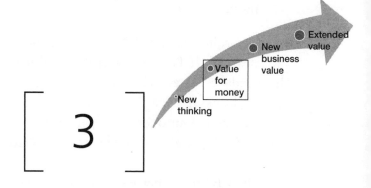

[3]

Show Value for Money

The waste of money cures itself, for soon there is no more to waste.

—M. W. Harrison

ONE OF THE BEST CIOs we know shared a story of his first CIO assignment. He had painstakingly prepared a presentation for the senior team describing how IT could be more strategic to the company. He was arguing that IT could create efficiencies and synergies that would pay off in new competitive advantages for the company. All it would take was for the company to restructure its old systems and processes, and to give him a "seat at the table" for its strategic conversations.

About five minutes into the presentation, he saw that the audience was cold and silent. Realizing that his message was falling on deaf ears, he decided to wrap up quickly and wait for a better opportunity.

Soon after, in a conversation with one of the business unit chiefs who'd been present, he asked what was behind the cold reception. The answer was direct and memorable. "You can't run your own business," the executive said. "Why would I let you touch mine?"

According to the CIO, it was the most important lesson he ever learned. If IT was not visibly well managed—if costs were high and service levels low, as was the perceived case at the time—he would never have the credibility to influence the rest of the organization. Improving IT's performance would show he had the leadership and change management credentials required of a business leader.

The CIO took that lesson to heart, resolving to improve the performance of the IT unit at his company. It was a lesson he took with him as he moved on to subsequent CIO and CIO-plus positions at higher levels of authority.

Show value for money before you try to prove that IT is an investment in future business performance.

When the enterprise's IT organization delivers value for money, the enterprise is getting the quality of IT service it needs at a competitive price—and everyone knows it. In effect, this means that the IT organization is performing these essential functions well enough to be the preferred alternative to any competent external supplier.

This is the necessary starting point for recognition of the value IT contributes to the enterprise. If the enterprise doesn't know that IT is delivering value for money, no further discussion of value is possible.

If the door is closed, that's how to open it.

Value for money *means that the IT organization is providing the right services, at the right level of quality, at a competitive price—and the rest of the business knows it.*

There are three essential steps to delivering value for money:

1. Measure and communicate IT's performance in terms that are meaningful to the rest of the business.

2. Benchmark IT's performance against peers.

3. Provide data that will help the rest of the enterprise manage consumption of IT services.

Let's discuss each of these steps in order.

Measure and communicate IT's performance

Although there is much of value in life and business that can't be measured, it remains true that what is not measured can't be improved. By measuring and communicating its performance in terms that are meaningful to the rest of the business—and following up to improve the performance areas that are lagging—IT shows that it is serious about strengthening its capabilities and delivering better value for money every day.

On the other hand, if the metrics to prove value for money aren't there, then executives (understandably) are likely to believe that IT can't deliver, at which point the IT organization has fallen squarely into a value trap. The perception that IT can't deliver might or might not be accurate, but if no one can say for sure, then the perception is probably true.

Players know the score

Every executive in the world knows that if you don't know what the score is, you're not a player. Top performers always know what their numbers are. To be perceived as a top performer, IT must know the score and communicate it to the rest of the business—just as the head of sales knows and communicates the sales figures for the latest quarter.

"IT needs internal operational metrics. And these metrics need to be founded on something solid. Without that, it's an exercise in bluffing and misdirection."[1]

—Guido Sacchi, CEO, Moneta Corporation (former CIO, CompuCredit)

Not just any measures of performance will do

Recall that delivering only technology is one of the value traps. Measurements of IT performance must be meaningful to business executives who know little or nothing about technology (and who rightly should not need to know in order to understand IT's performance). It's easy for IT leaders to forget that and report on performance in machine-centric terms, not least because the machine-centric numbers are readily available and widely used within IT.

As an example of communication that destroys perception of IT value, consider the metrics in table 3-1, which are taken from an IT department's monthly report to the executive team at an anonymous company.

All these metrics, without exception, are about machine performance. As such, they should never have been shown to anyone except the technicians responsible for maintaining the systems. There's nothing in the chart that would help any executive outside IT know the impact of IT's performance on the rest of the business. The goal metrics for availability, a measure of service quality, apparently were not met in two of five categories—in one case, they were off by about 10 percent—but what does that mean to anyone outside IT? What business functions were affected when availability declined, with what outcomes? For that matter, what were the actual goals, as opposed to the percentage of goal achieved? On those points the chart is mute. The clear implication

TABLE 3-1

An IT department's monthly performance report to management

Performance measure *System reliability*	Percent of scheduled availability
LAN connectivity	>=97.9%
UNIX	>=99%
Oracle database	>=99%
Paging	>=91%
Phone switch	>=99%

is that the IT organization is concerned only with the performance of its machines and not at all with the performance of the business.

The right metrics are about quality and price for visible services

The measurements used to show value for money must communicate that IT is providing the right services, at the right level of quality, at the right price.

- *The right services* are critical to business performance and are visible in some way to users. The right services might be as simple as e-mail or as complex as an infrastructure upgrade.

- *The right level of quality* means that the business gets the quality of service it needs. It doesn't pay for more than is necessary, and it doesn't get lower quality than needed when lower quality has an unacceptable impact on business performance.

- *The right price* means that IT's services are competitively *unit priced* (priced per unit of service delivered).

Finally, because almost everyone in the business uses IT, IT's metrics must help everyone use IT better. Measures aren't meaningful unless they can influence behavior, which in turn influences the total cost of IT. This is a critical point, and one to which we return later in this chapter.

The best metrics for IT to use in communicating with the rest of the business about IT's performance in returning value for money meet all these criteria. For example, table 3-2 shows metrics shared by Sam Coursen, CIO of Freescale Semiconductor, in a presentation to an industry conference in October 2007.

These services aren't necessarily the ones that every IT organization would choose to report on. Some of these metrics could be

TABLE 3-2

IT metrics at Freescale Semiconductor

IT services	Cost metrics	Service level metrics
PCs	• Cost per PC • Desktop/laptop ratio	• Time to install • Time to resolve problems
E-mail	• Cost per mailbox • Mailboxes	• Availability • Message delivery time
Help desk	• Cost per contact • Contacts/user	• Time to resolve problems • User satisfaction
Infrastructure services • Voice network • Data network • Servers • Telecom	• Total cost = Unit cost × volume	• Availability • Performance
Business applications	• Cost/function point • Cost by business area	Projects • Delivery to schedule • Delivery to budget • Defects in production Support • Time to resolve problems

Source: Sam Coursen, Freescale Semiconductor, "Building World-Class IT at Freescale," industry presentation, October 2007. Used by permission.

improved (such as substituting hours of downtime, which can more easily be converted to business impact, for availability percentage). But they have certain characteristics that make them good candidates for most organizations.

- They are visible to the rest of the business, either directly (because they are used by business unit personnel) or indirectly (because employees are dependent on the service to enable things that they touch—for example, application development). In other words, these services matter to the rest of the business.

- Costs are measured as unit costs rather than overall budget or cost levels.

- Quality is measured in ways that are meaningful and material to the business.

- The metrics transparently show both unit costs and consumption.

- They are significant components of the overall cost of IT at Freescale.

- They can be compared to external benchmarks, which Freescale obtains from three companies: Compass, Hackett, and Gartner, Inc.

Note that the services listed in the Freescale chart generally do not tie directly to revenue. (The obvious exception is business applications.) It is not possible to determine which revenues result directly from good e-mail or voice network service. These are examples of what are typically called run-the-business, lights on, or sustaining services—services that are essential to the functioning of the business or to reducing business risk but do not tie directly to revenue streams. Examples of run-the-business services in non-IT functions include human resources or audit and regulatory compliance; other examples in IT include information security and patch management tools.

For run-the-business services, the measure of value is always based on achieving the best possible balance between price (usually unit cost) and performance (including quality). These metrics are represented in the Freescale chart in table 3-2 by the columns headed "Cost metrics" and "Service level metrics." The goal, in value-for-money terms, is not necessarily to have the world's best performance or the world's lowest cost, but to have the right mix of cost and quality for the enterprise. The service level and resulting cost may vary by business unit, by IT service, or by business process. But everyone should be able to agree that the IT unit is providing the right mix for each part of the business that it serves. (A simple test is to see whether everyone would agree on an answer to the following question: "For this IT service, is it worth investing $xx to improve performance by yy%?")

JM Family Enterprises is a $10.1 billion (2008) diversified private automotive company. Its principal businesses focus on vehicle distribution and processing, financial services, finance and insurance products, retail sales, marketing and consulting, and dealer technology products and services. The enterprise has been cited as a top company to work for by *Fortune* and *Computer World* magazines.

In 2005, the enterprise's VP of technology operations, Tom Holmes, developed a dashboard that links IT technology performance to business process performance. It shows, in real time, how service levels on networks and servers translate to transaction speed and business process performance, and then to performance of each business unit and the enterprise as a whole. At any moment, IT or business executives can look at the dashboards on the wall and understand whether their part of the business is running at 100 percent. When the network slows down, or when a server runs into trouble, everyone can see what part of the business is affected and by how much.

According to Holmes, "Instead of saying that the mainframe is up, the Sun servers are up, both routers are up, and so on, it says that contract sales are up. This system is really changing the whole mindset of the IT shop." The point is important. The metrics IT chooses to report send messages to IT personnel as well as to the rest of the business. "As business and technology complexity increases, the dashboard has created a common language across IT and the business," according to Rajeev Ravindran, CTO of JM Family.[2]

The dashboard is visible on a big screen outside the company's executive suites as well as being prominently displayed inside the CIO's office. Every time an executive gets off the elevator, he or she sees how the dials are performing. Because the numbers usually look good, they reinforce executives' perceptions that the IT unit is doing a solid job of powering their business operations.

An electronic display outside the executive offices certainly isn't a mandatory channel for communicating IT's value. Some cultures might find it ostentatious, to the point of offensiveness. But in this case, it communicates visibly that there's a real player on the field, which is exactly what a scoreboard is supposed to do.

IT is now viewed as a business peer with comparable metrics and business goals.

Why unit cost per service is important

Some CIOs report costs only at an aggregate level—such as IT cost as a percentage of revenue—rather than on detailed numbers that describe costs on a per-service-unit basis, such as the cost of supporting a desktop. This practice is a mistake, because the numbers are aggregated at a level too high to guide action. IT spend as a percentage of revenue is an all-encompassing number that incorporates many complexities in types and volume of services delivered, as well as ways the enterprise uses IT in the business. It says almost nothing about the underlying factors that influence change, so it's useless for understanding changes in IT spend from year to year even within the same enterprise.

Unit cost per service is a far better metric. It provides information that everyone can use to assess and improve IT value for money. It is readily comparable across enterprises, and even across parts of the same enterprise. At the very least it enables meaningful year-on-year comparisons inside the same enterprise.

Such measures also help IT make the case that value-for-money performance is improving. As Celanese CIO Karl Wachs says, "My favorite graph is the one that shows costs going down and service levels going up."[3] In a fast-growing enterprise, this graph can help show why IT budgets, though rising, are nevertheless money well spent.

Figure 3-1 shows how a fast-rising IT budget in State Street Corporation looked when presented in unit costs per business transaction instead of pure spending numbers. State Street provides investment services, investment management, trading, and research to corporations, mutual funds, pension funds, and other clients. It is a world leader in servicing mutual funds, servicing and managing pension assets, and foreign exchange. IT is critical to State Street's businesses, and the company's IT budget reflects the importance.

FIGURE 3-1

IT spend metrics at a fast-growing company

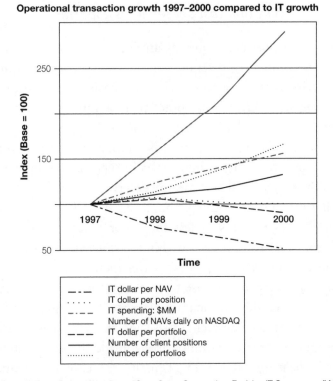

Operational transaction growth 1997–2000 compared to IT growth

Source: Peter Weill and Richard Woodham, "State Street Corporation: Evolving IT Governance," MIT CISR
Working paper #327, August 2002.

As the figure shows, IT spending increased by approximately
50 percent from 1997 to 2000. But, during the same period, the
number of portfolios serviced increased at about the same rate,
and the number of net asset value (NAV) calculations nearly
tripled. While State Street's IT spending was increasing quickly, so
was the company's transaction volume.

Plotting the unit cost ratios of IT spend versus NAV, portfolio,
or position tells a different story than the one told by the upward-
sloping IT spending line. IT spending per portfolio or position
stayed roughly constant over the time period. And IT spending
per NAV decreased significantly during the period. This is the

power of unit cost analysis instead of simple budget numbers. It accounts for growth in the business and shows where IT is generating economies of scale. Unit costs are also comparable across divisions and companies, providing further information to assess performance.

As every CIO knows, for technology-based IT services, industrywide technology trends tend to reduce unit costs over time. Increased usage volume can also reduce the unit costs of most fixed technology investments. In other words, trends within and outside the enterprise usually work in favor of the IT organization's unit costs. The CIO can choose when and how to have the discussion about whether those costs are dropping fast enough for the enterprise—whether the enterprise needs to reduce particular costs at a rate faster than the industry. For example, Google's infrastructure in 2007 included an addressable memory space one billion times as large as the space addressed by IBM's "Big Blue" computer in 1998. During this same period, Moore's law alone produced an increase by a factor of 64. Clearly, progress at everyone else's rate wasn't enough for Google.

Use metrics like a manager, not an engineer, to turn IT around

In metrics, as in many other things, the perfect is the enemy of the good. Executives drive their businesses by using a host of imprecise but useful metrics. IT can operate in the same way. But IT professionals as a group are much like engineers, and engineers think differently from managers. Engineers want perfection. Managers want something that works. Engineers want everything to run smoothly at launch. Managers want it to be better today than it was yesterday, every day. They know perfection is not possible, but small improvements add up to dramatic improvements over time. In this regard as in many others, CIOs need to think like managers and not like engineers.

Kevin Vasconi is CIO of Michigan-based R.L. Polk & Co., a privately held enterprise with global operations that provides market information to the automotive industry. Given the nature of Polk's business, IT is critical to success and growth. But that doesn't mean IT has always been highly regarded at the company. "When I arrived in 2002," says Vasconi, "IT had an execution problem. But in the first couple of weeks, I found that the executive team expected me to do more than manage IT costs. IT needed to contribute significantly to the business. I needed to fix IT and get us to higher value, to grow revenue via technology."[4]

A key contributor to "fixing IT" was an extensive metrics program. "We had to identify our problems objectively," Vasconi says. "At first, there was suspicion. But then senior management started to see improvements in the data. It's now one of the strongest tools I have. We always begin discussions with the data."

Vasconi's team uses the following IT measures to demonstrate progress in performance:

- *Uptime,* which is equivalent to sales and service channel availability in a business where the product is delivered to customers electronically on demand

- *Application performance,* such as the time needed for an application to respond to a request from a user, another metric that is highly visible to internal users as well as external customers

- *On-time project delivery,* a critical metric for product availability in a company whose products are information based

- *On-budget project delivery*

- *"First time right" application development*

- *Cost-saving opportunities,* an important metric in a business where IT is a significant portion of all costs, and a useful measure for many infrastructure investments

- *Software quality* based on defects per thousand lines of code, an important measure of product quality in a software-driven business

Note the similarity of many of these metrics to Coursen's model, and the visibility of the performance to the business in every case. "These metrics are the table stakes," says Vasconi. "If you can't do them well, you can't get to the next stage. You can't have a conversation around cost until you've had the conversation around operations, because cost is irrelevant until you've solved the operational problems."

Vasconi's story, down to the last comment, is echoed by Randy Spratt of McKesson: "Initially, we had to assess the IT operation and build the relationships we needed to operate successfully as a business. Many of those relationships were with our internal customer base—the McKesson businesses. Then we needed to work to fix the issues, which were about cost, quality, value, transparency. Then we had to show our plans to fix the issues, then we had to execute on the plans. Like any business, you've got a brief honeymoon period where you show people you're going to improve their issues, and then you have to deliver."[5]

Benchmark IT's performance against peers

Every executive and investor in the world accepts without question the notion that a business's performance is meaningful only when measured against that of its competitors. In other words, business executives routinely expect their performance to be measured against external peers. To argue that it should it be different for the business executive who runs IT is to invite suspicion from the executive team.

"Everything you do in a business involves benchmarking your capabilities against your competitors."[6]

—Randy Spratt, CIO, McKesson

Our research has convinced us that in most cases, neither the CIO nor the rest of the executive team can know for sure whether the IT function is providing a competitive unit price for any given level of quality without benchmarking the IT team's performance against peer companies. In the absence of direct comparisons, no one can say definitively whether IT's performance in either quality or cost is weak or world-class or anything in between. And we are certain that in this situation most executives simply assume that their IT is not world-class, whether or not they think it's "good enough." Almost every one of the highly effective CIOs we interviewed for this research benchmarks IT cost and quality of service against peer companies every twelve to twenty-four months. (Benchmarking more frequently than that leaves little time for implementing improvements and measuring the effects.)

There are important exceptions to this rule. First, if the CIO and executive team are satisfied that unit costs and quality are competitive—in other words, that value for money has been achieved—then benchmarking those factors may not be the best use of the IT organization's time and attention. The same is true in many fast-growing companies where management is much less concerned about unit costs than about putting all available resources into meeting demand.

But even fast-growing companies need to keep score at some point. The CIO of A_Soft_Co (not the real company name), a software company with sales of nearly $300 million in 2007, found that benchmarking was essential to managing executive perception of IT costs. "We suffered . . . from 'mom and pop' syndrome," says the CIO. "We didn't really have a defined approach to growth. I wasn't asked to do benchmarking originally. I was asked to help the company grow. But we realized quickly that we needed to be able to show that we were spending in the right way." The company's IT spend more than doubled from 2005 to 2008. "As I started increasing budget, I needed to show that this was what businesses generally spent on IT." The second exception involves the availability of peers for benchmarking. If it is difficult to find comparable peers for the IT organization, the value of benchmarking is diminished. We have encountered IT organizations whose operations are unique, such as the membership organization whose IT team was responsible for supporting tens of thousands of volunteers running personally selected and configured computers in the field. Help desk costs for this organization were high compared with most, but an extensive benchmarking exercise didn't show much that wasn't already known about the situation. In this case, it's more fruitful for the IT organization to compare its own performance year over year, within and across IT organizational units. This practice doesn't demonstrate that IT is cost effective compared with peers and competitors, but it offers the opportunity to (visibly) measure improvements in performance.

CIOs should be careful about assuming too quickly that their operations have no peers. All companies are different, and CIOs who do extensive benchmarking will often be the first to acknowledge that benchmarking does not allow for perfect comparison. However, the same CIOs will say that they are able to benefit far more from their benchmarks, even with their imperfections, than from not having any external comparisons for making decisions. They take pains to benchmark IT services that are most comparable across organizations, to use unit costs and standard performance and satisfaction measures. And they are careful to analyze any differences between their firms and benchmarks to understand whether they reflect differences in performance or just differences in the companies.

A third exception is that benchmarking is not necessarily the best use of IT resources when specific areas of performance are obviously in need of improvement. In particular, if the CIO finds that IT processes are so immature or unstable that it's difficult even to gather data about process performance, then the best approach is to take immediate steps to improve those processes. (To put it another way, if the process is almost impossible to measure, you don't need a benchmark to tell you that it needs a lot of improvement.) Benchmarking can follow when the processes are stabilized enough to make data gathering feasible.

"If the processes are like a black box, it's hard to do a benchmark—too much work, not enough outcome. If you've just joined the company, set up the processes that will allow you to collect the data."[7]

—Daniel Janeba, CIO, Zentiva

A process for making a go–no go decision on benchmarking is depicted in figure 3-2.

In addition to these exceptions, we offer a further caveat, which is that benchmarks do not answer certain questions that are very important to everyone involved in a business, such as, "What is the right level of IT spend, in what areas, for my business?" and "What is the value contributed by IT to my business?" Benchmarks describe costs and quality; whether the relative levels

FIGURE 3-2

A decision process on benchmarking

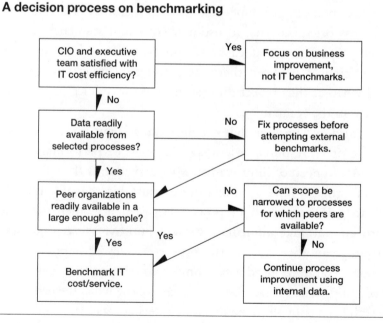

of costs and quality are appropriate is another question. For example, one CIO we know was concerned that 75 percent of his budget was consumed by infrastructure and operations. It turned out that his $1 billion company's value proposition demanded absolutely reliable twenty-four-hour service to customers in multiple locations globally, which in turn required plenty of infrastructure in multiple locations to ensure global uptime. The company's infrastructure and operations were well managed for both costs and quality. Given those facts, the only realistic option to significantly reduce the percentage of the budget devoted to infrastructure was to increase the overall size of the budget. None of this was shown by the benchmark on its face—all that appeared there was the discrepancy between their infrastructure spend and that of their similarly sized peers. In this sense it's good to keep in mind, as one CIO told us, that "it's a measurement tool, not a marketing tool," and measurements must always be put in context.

Exceptions and caveats aside, for most IT organizations, benchmarking is a useful tool for establishing value for money. Randy Spratt, CIO of McKesson, describes how benchmarking against industry peers influenced IT's turnaround in the company:

> The benchmarks [that we did in 2006] matched our costs and quality of service against industry practices and the likely cost to outsource those functions. We took the results of that series of benchmarks and prioritized them into the areas where we had the largest gaps, then assessed the strategy we should take to close those gaps. We brought a series of initiatives and investments to our newly formed governance board to show them how we would address the gaps and bring IT performance to world-class levels of quality and cost. We successfully used a surgical mix of strategies— some outsourcing, some smart sourcing, some internal improvements.
>
> We've addressed many of the issues around fragmented procurement costs, cost structure around server administration, and the management of a fragmented security environment.

We're just now receiving approval for a large-scale data center consolidation that will significantly reduce data center costs. So we've shown that we can manage IT effectively.[8]

Spratt's remarks foreshadow the natural progression from IT as a source of value for money to IT as an investment in future business performance—the subject we turn to in the next chapter. Spratt concludes, "We've also inserted ourselves into business planning at the strategic level and the operational level. We've established a trusted relationship with IT, and the business is increasingly willing to turn to IT to help them solve the technical problems behind their strategies. We're becoming essentially an IT consultant to the business, climbing the value chain."

Benchmarking was a key factor in the turnaround of Intel's IT

Many CIOs might enviously assume that Intel's IT unit would get much more respect from business executives than their own unit gets. After all, Intel's products power much of the world's IT infrastructure; how could its IT team be anything but celebrated and revered in the company? But Intel's culture is dominated by its engineering and sales units, and in such businesses internal functions like IT, finance, and HR often play subsidiary support roles on behalf of highly informed and demanding internal customers. Such customers run their own operations by the numbers, and they have little patience for anyone who can't. As mentioned in chapter 1, Intel's IT, which had limited visibility into its own performance in the late 1990s, was the unhappy target of internal jokes about its quality, high costs, and limited delivery capabilities.

CIO Doug Busch accepted responsibility for transforming the substance and perception of IT's performance. Busch and his team started the transformation by identifying a set of core IT services and benchmarking performance against other enterprises

FIGURE 3-3

Intel's unit cost/quality matrix

2003 IT benchmarks: How our products and services compare

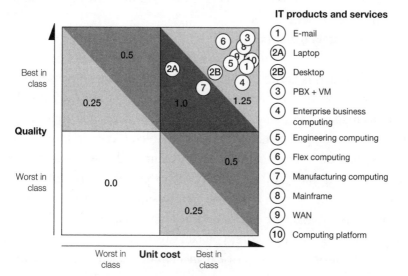

Intel IT conducts detailed benchmarking with a consortium of peer IT organizations. We compare cost and quality for our highest impact products and services. In 2003, benchmarking results showed continued improvement in absolute terms, and strong relative quality and cost results for each product or service.

Source: Intel IT Annual Performance Report, www.intel.com. Used by permission.

in the industry. Figure 3-3 shows an example of one of the key charts Busch used to demonstrate IT's performance and improve the way he related to his business counterparts. This chart shows a simple ranking of IT's performance in eleven key areas on the axes of quality and unit cost as compared with those of a consortium of peer organizations.[9]

It would be anyone's pleasure to show this figure to the CEO; it demonstrates that in all services measured, Intel IT's unit costs and quality are among the best in the peer group. Note also that the chart describes performance for services considered by the organization to be the most important provided by IT. In almost every case, these metrics are related to services that touch users directly. Other value-for-money metrics reported by IT separately include delivery against internal targets and external promises in areas such as cost, service quality, project delivery, and business customer satisfaction targets. These are also measures of services that users experience directly.

When Intel IT first published this report in 1999, most services were rated poorly on one or more dimensions. But this chart and the others in this series changed the nature of the conversation. Each iteration of the reports improved the credibility of Busch and his management team in the eyes of their peers and superiors. Factual data on performance and cost enabled fact-based, rational discussions of where to target investment and effort—a much more focused and productive approach than previous conversations (and arguments) based on impressions and assumptions, in which the highest priorities and needs were always in dispute. (If you don't know the score, you can't be a player.)

These measures were critical in helping Busch and his team make better business decisions when transforming the organization. By consolidating infrastructure, improving measurement, creating transparent governance mechanisms, and continuously improving core processes, the IT unit changed both the reality and the perception of its service delivery. Total cost of ownership for PCs was reduced more than 50 percent. Infrastructure unit cost and service quality improved significantly compared with external benchmarks. Customer satisfaction improved, with more than 80 percent of internal customers rating IT as a strategic business partner (as opposed to a technology expert/provider or vendor) by 2003. These improvements were accomplished while the overall IT budget was reduced in absolute terms as well as a percentage of revenue.

By then, IT and business executives were able to focus on bigger fish. Performance was visibly improved and was still improving, and the executives trusted Busch to make good decisions on how to continuously improve it. The executive team's time devoted to IT was better spent on how to use IT for competitive advantage. Even though the enterprise continually tries to keep IT costs as low as possible, it also is finding more ways to use IT to improve business operations.

The epilogue to this story is that the metrics-based improvement process was also good for the IT team and its leaders. Busch left IT to become the technology leader for one of Intel's new business units. The IT team built on the credibility it had gained by improving infrastructure delivery and began improving the way it measured project value and prioritized projects. And from there it took on a bigger challenge—helping improve the innovativeness not only of the IT unit but also of the enterprise as a whole. Taking on this role—a critical one in a company that dominates its markets through innovation in products and operations—would have been unthinkable even five years before. In short, by focusing on metrics even when IT performance was poor, Intel was able to improve its IT performance. Everybody won.

Start benchmarking where you are,
not where you'd like to be

Benchmarking begins with internal analysis. Sam Coursen of Freescale describes his company's process:

> We did a breakdown of the services we provide, and the costs for those services. Then we benchmarked externally to help us figure out where we were off the mark.
>
> Being able to show where we stand compared to benchmarks helps to demonstrate the value proposition and show where we can improve. The first two years I was here, I reduced the IT budget by five percent per year. Now we're doing a major supply chain project with SAP, which is pushing the budget up again. I tell the CFO and the CEO we've already paid for it.
>
> To do the benchmarking, we used two different service providers: an external service we'd used before, and another group with a very rigorous IT cost model. One of the problems with IT cost is that people quote what their cost is, but

you never know what costs are included. Are cell phones included, for example? What's good about a precise cost model is that you know everyone in your peer group is including the same cost elements. So we used that model for the overall spend benchmark and got a report saying how we compared to other companies of our size and footprint.

With our other benchmarking provider, we went through a service-by-service review, with very detailed breakdowns of costs in the unit categories. For example, how much does it cost to solve a help desk ticket, and how many am I solving? Sometimes your unit cost is off benchmark; sometimes it's your quantities that are off benchmark. Help desk is a good example. If you have a good infrastructure, you might get less than one help desk call per user per month. If you have a complex infrastructure, you might get twice that.[10]

Wherever you have to start measuring, start

The head of a cardiology practice we know tried to incent his doctors to keep cholesterol under control in their patients. He wanted to make cholesterol control a part of every doctor's annual performance review.

He met with plenty of resistance. Every doctor thought his patients were tougher to manage than anyone else's. Some doctors argued that total cholesterol was a bad number to use, worse than no number at all.

The CEO took another tack. He asked his administrators to make a simple change in the medical charts each patient got at each office visit: writing the patient's total cholesterol count at the top of the chart. No incentives, no rules—only information. Total cholesterol count is only a proxy for better health, but the number was available and, most would argue, at least somewhat relevant.

After a year, the practice saw a huge improvement in the percentage of patients whose cholesterol was under control. The doctors started informally competing to see whose office had better cholesterol performance, and this competition improved the numbers even more.

The doctors had used many arguments to resist being held accountable, but in the end the number, imperfect as it was, became part of their thinking and part of the conversation. Each patient, and each doctor, was unique, but the doctors found a way to agree on a set of metrics and to use them to improve performance. The total cholesterol count number was not the only one the doctors used, but all of them used that one. And as a result, patient health improved.

There are a few important lessons in this story.

- Don't let the search for the perfect number keep you from using a useful, if imperfect, metric.

- Most people, when given information in a form they can use, will take it into account and change their decisions accordingly.

- When comparisons are available, people will compare themselves to others, and that can help everyone improve.

The CIO of A_Soft_Co (the software company mentioned previously) has established eight areas for ongoing benchmarks:

1. *Cost controls.*

2. *Operational excellence.* Sample metrics include the following:

   - Average resolution time for service requests, which is broken down by problem type and service request. "A problem is something different from a service request—from someone who wants you to do something for them," says the CIO.

   - Number of critical outages—how many planned and unplanned? "We track how many hours systems are available for use. So we take a penalty on maintenance windows as well."

3. *Financial controls.* "These are about deviations," the CIO says. "For example, percent of capital and operational spend deviation—what's my variance? This is about planning to manage, and managing to plan. It's me against myself. This helps us think ahead and prevent surprises for the rest of the business. I have three CFOs on top of me, so I get the flavor of what they pick on. IT spend as a percentage of revenue, IT OpEx [operating expenses], and IT spend per seat are how we're homing in on the way we're spending money."

4. *Human capital.* Sample metrics include these:

   • IT head count by department. "I want to see head count shrink by the end of the quarter, and know how many people are available to do certain work."

   • Turnover rate.

   • Time required to fill an open requisition, by manager.

5. *Customer satisfaction.* Sample metrics include these:

   • User ratings of the support experience: helpfulness of the help desk technician, timeliness of issue resolution, whether the user was informed of progress while resolution was under way.

   • Unstructured user comments. "What we found is that it's important to collect comments," says the CIO. "You find out more about what can be improved in the comments than anywhere else."

6. *Business impact and alignment.* Sample metrics include these:

   • Percent of IT staff working on new development projects: "ERP, sales automation, any type of business process facing work."

   • Percentage of IT cost by line of business.

- Degree of IT participation in business planning processes.

- Maintenance and enhancement as percentages of the development budget. "We find that we're continuously spending more money on operations, as compared to applications."

7. *Application development.* Sample metrics include these:

   - Project scope, schedule, and cost. "We look for percentage of on-time delivery and resource variance for the highest-value projects—not all projects," the CIO says. "If it's not consequential to the business, we don't care about it. Getting better formats on a report doesn't matter; getting more accurate and timely billing does. We stack rank our projects on business value using several criteria—growing revenue, process improvement, scalability (up or down), cost reduction—and combine them for our total value score. Some people recommended we look at eleven or fifteen factors, but these are the ones that matter."

   - Technology. "How often does a new project include a new technology?"

8. *Capacity planning.* "This is the most boring of all," the CIO says. But it's clearly important in a business where the IT budget has more than doubled in three years.

Freescale's and A_Soft_Co's approaches are detailed and comprehensive, but benchmarking need not be perfect or expensive. Some firms have the benefit of a nonprofit industry group to help in the benchmarking, but other enterprises get benchmarking through for-profit consultants. External benchmarking suppliers quote prices as low as $30,000–$50,000 to compare standard IT service costs and quality across their benchmark samples. Indepth analyses can cost more, but the buyer can choose how much or how little depth is necessary. Note that as per Coursen's comments, one of the key value-adds brought by benchmarking consultants is their extensive databases of metrics and companies, something that simplifies decisions about what data to gather and increases the usefulness of the data that is gathered.

What if you can't afford even $50,000 for an external benchmark? Start by benchmarking against yourself, as State Street Corporation did (see figure 3-1, presented earlier). How are your unit cost and service levels this year compared with previous years? How do services and costs vary by business unit or geography within your enterprise? In many cases, your IT unit already has the numbers you need if you dig into old budgets, bills, and logs.

Peter Bennington, CIO for the City of Stirling, Australia, used his experience to design a benchmarking survey and enlisted other Australian cities in the effort.

> I started the process by getting support from the local CIO group. The process of engaging twenty local government agencies and getting them all signed up took the better part of a month. It didn't take a long time to put together the data collection form—a week's worth of work—because I'd done it previously in the state government. It took three months to chase down all the data; some people were too busy to get it. When you do analysis, that raises more questions. It took a couple of weeks to analyze all the data, then three weeks of my time to write up the report. Coming up with the key conclusions took time—only half a page, but a lot of thinking. End to end, it took me the best part of five to six months elapsed time. I was the only resource on it, and I was running a business unit IT group at the same time.
>
> But it was worth the time. I get fewer and fewer arguments now. When I do my year-to-year budget, now I can talk about industry benchmarks and what peer councils do. If I didn't do that, they'd just look at a big number and say, "Why are we spending that much on IT?" Now I can point

to spend to revenue, capital operating budgets, and so on, which gives me lots of credibility. It helps me justify additional staff; our staffing ratios are less than similarly sized organizations. I won't underspend, and I won't go to the top either. We look at other parameters, too, like implementing ITIL [IT Infrastructure Library]. Only 30 percent of public agencies surveyed have a project management methodology, so we're outstripping them.

When the CEO says, "This local council is doing some interesting stuff here. What are we doing?" I can say, "They're doing that because they have more staff in that area than us." I'm on the front foot now, not the back foot. I can deal with the rumor-mongering.[11]

The important thing is to start, even if perfect numbers aren't available. The absence of perfect metrics didn't stop Guido Sacchi at CompuCredit or Kevin Vasconi at R.L. Polk from communicating successfully about value for money. Nor did Tom Holmes at JM Family spend millions of dollars or months of staff time gathering requirements for his dashboard system. It was treated as a research and development effort utilizing reinvestment dollars. Realizing it would be nearly impossible to build the perfect dashboard, he decided to build something quickly and then tune it. He gathered a few people in a conference room to build a prototype, then began demonstrating the prototype to selected audiences. The IT team initially had to guess at the weightings that connected each level of technology to every other, and ultimately to business processes. But having a starting point helped start conversations about those connections, and the conversations helped them refine the accuracy of the system over time. According to Ravindran, now IT and the business speak in terms of business services instead of technical jargon.

In other words, starting now with the best available metrics is the path not only to improving performance but also to getting better metrics to improve performance even more.

Help the rest of the enterprise use IT well

Benchmarking helps the whole business understand how well IT is performing, whether compared to external peers or to its own past performance. And the importance of benchmarking is hard to overstate, given that it's about goals, transparency, and credibility for IT, and about time and money for everyone else. But there's more to defining the right price than calculating unit costs, no matter how well unit costs compare to peers. As Sam Coursen told us, "Total costs are the product of unit costs (the rate) times volume. The business end of the costs is the volume side. If you have all the data, you can attack both unit costs and volume issues."

In other words, to keep IT costs under control—to deliver the right services at the right price—IT must help people throughout the business make good decisions about how they use IT. This is critical: the metrics IT uses to communicate value for money must help the rest of the business become smart IT consumers.

This is not the same thing as making smart decisions about investments in IT. Rather, it's about making smart consumption decisions—decisions about costs, not return on equity (ROE) or return on investment (ROI). You do it by making the factors that drive costs visible to the people who can use that information to control costs—in many cases, individual users of IT services.

Coursen continues:

When I came to Freescale, everybody had a pager—HR people were getting paged out of meetings. I asked, "Why?" So we collected thousands of pagers. Costs went down by millions of dollars, and most of the people involved had never wanted a pager in the first place.

I got a cell phone, but I never saw the bill. Our vendors were giving us paper, which makes it hard to analyze the cost. We got the vendors to give us the data, so we could charge by use and send every user in the company the details on their own consumption. As we decomposed everything into services with total cost equal to rate times volume, we tried to change the way people were charged to what we called "line of sight." That means you get charged only for what you use, and if you can figure out how to be efficient and not use it, you don't get the charge.

We gave them data they can use to manage their own performance—the data they can use to impact their own behavior.[12]

At JM Family, IT/business relationship managers bring charge-back reports to meetings with their business unit counterparts that show the overall bill, by service, for the business unit. They also show unit costs and usage volume for each service. Each service is rated with a "variability index" that indicates how much of the cost can be changed by modifying usage of the service. Costs for services rated a 1 (for example, the cost of a network connection) change very little with user behavior. But costs for a level-5 service are largely under the user's control. For example, printing costs can be reduced by "printing" to electronic media (such as a PDF file or electronic bill), or by printing differently (in black and white versus color, or printing on two sides). All are choices the user can make. And where services whose variability index are rated level 1 are beyond the control of the business unit, IT relationship managers show how much the IT unit is doing to keep those costs reasonable. The data provided by the chargeback reports helps the business units identify the best opportunities for managing their IT costs, and helps explain why less-variable unit costs are priced as they are. Ravindran summarizes, "Four years

---

"When you start talking from the same playbook, things change. As we get better with communicating costs in terms of actual activities, we can have a much more intelligent conversation when we are asked to provide 'off-the-menu' services."[13]

—Cara Schnaper, EVP, Technology & Operations, TIAA-CREF

"We opened up our finances and made them transparent. In mid-2006 we delivered a one-line allocation to the business. Now we deliver a complete invoice. Between transparency, benchmarking, and competitive bid efforts, we have strengthened the view that our finances are under control, we're driving to continual improvement on a per-unit cost basis, and we hold ourselves accountable for delivering to service levels.

"We don't hear, 'Why does IT cost so much?' now. Do we still have expense-level conversations? Yes, but they're more about how we can jointly reduce costs."[14]

—Randy Spratt, CIO, McKesson

after implementation, IT costs have now been made more transparent to the business at the service level, driving improved decision making."[15]

By creating transparent, ongoing reporting about the performance of IT services, the CIO changes the nature of the conversation about IT spend. Instead of asking, "Why does IT cost so much?" executives ask, "Are we getting the right services and quality for a good price? What can my business unit do to help control our IT costs?"

Putting it together: One company's example

InfoInfinity (a pseudonym) is a multibillion-dollar information broker. Its IT unit is seen as performing poorly, delivering neither adequate service levels nor value. A few months ago, following a merger with a competitor, a new CIO was appointed. He is justifiably concerned because IT's performance is visibly lagging, and he's now responsible for improving it.

An ongoing issue is that the company's new products are introduced without warning to IT, forcing a scramble to build the necessary support systems and infrastructure. Because the company's products are data intensive and there are many buyers (who purchase access via subscription), a new product might mean a sudden surge in demand for IT infrastructure and services. Satisfying this demand ad hoc is expensive and difficult. These results guarantee ongoing dissatisfaction with IT. Company executives feel that the 10 percent of revenue spent on IT should deliver more value faster.

The IT team understands key aspects of the dilemma. In particular, team members recognize that they have not succeeded in demonstrating value for money. They are taking steps to improve IT architecture (to reduce needless variations in technology that have produced excess cost and increased time to market), improve IT processes, and better manage demand (via IT governance). But they also believe that they need to do a better job communicating with the business about the value IT delivers.

Realizing that the IT team had not linked its performance to business performance, the CIO initiated an exercise to identify the top operational metrics for the business and then describe what IT needed to do to address those operational outcomes. In thirty minutes of discussion, the IT leadership team produced six key operational metrics, five financial metrics (included because they are part of the executive compensation plans and so drive executive behavior), and a few issues that complicate operations and measurement (such as the definition of revenue types—a task made difficult because of the complexity of the company's products and pricing schemes). In another twenty minutes, the team produced a description of what IT needed to do to support those operational and financial needs, generally mapping IT current and desired capabilities to the business outcomes. The results are shown in table 3-3, taken from the chart created by the team.

With this simple exercise completed, the team immediately saw the business value of its initiatives in a different light. For example, high systems availability has always been a given for the business, because products are delivered online. The operating assumption is that an online subscriber who can't get access to the

TABLE 3-3

Data broker: Most important operating metrics

Business outcomes	IT needs to support
• Net new subscription sales • Renewals • Ancillary revenue • Growth • Customer experience/satisfaction • Product stability/customer calls • Usage—number of concurrent users, disconnect rates	Availability Systems performance Lower rate of growth for IT cost IT more nimble Levers (shift money from other initia tives to IT) Rapid time to market Flexible options for levels of IT service

Issues

• Revenue recognition/analysis of revenue data
• Definition of what is new revenue
• Complexity of pricing (competitive advantage)

Financials

• Revenue (drives all compensation)
• Margins
• EPS (drives executive compensation)
• Return on invested capital (ROIC)

company's systems will immediately switch to a competitor. The team members saw that instead of simply saying, "We deliver high availability," they could connect high availability to the customer experience, to product usage (for which customers often pay extra in addition to their subscription fees), to customer retention, and ultimately to revenue. That insight shed a different light on the costs of high availability.

The IT team saw that it could make its business customers smarter consumers by explaining that "four nines" (99.99 percent) availability is sixteen times as expensive as "three nines" (99.9 percent availability).[16] It could then open a discussion about whether the desired outcomes—product usage and customer experience—were truly endangered by approaches that offered slightly lower guarantees of availability at lower cost, such as building multiple, less expensive data centers instead of one very-high-availability data center (an expense that rapid growth demanded frequently) to meet new product demand. This strategy would shift the conversation from "Why does IT cost so much?" to "Can we reduce or change systems performance requirements without jeopardizing the business outcomes we want?" The answer might be to retain the status quo—but the internal customers would know what they were paying for and would understand the value they were getting for their money.

This simple exercise was only the start of the work to be done, but it yielded valuable insights about how to change the IT team's thinking to relate its issues to what the business cared about. The kind of correlation made by the team needed to be extended out and down throughout the IT organization so that everyone in the organization understood which business outcomes were affected by IT's performance. This meant cultural change, which would probably take at least one or two years.

The team saw three major initiatives ahead in what was essentially equivalent to an IT turnaround:

- Improve IT management processes.

- Improve governance, primarily as a means to manage demand.

- Demonstrate value for money.

The IT leadership team realized that these initiatives could not be delivered unless it instilled its new mind-set in its units and in its business colleagues. The IT leaders needed to make all their IT initiatives relevant in business terms, and they needed to show their IT employees how to use that mind-set to guide their decisions and actions.[17]

This change is very new, and only time will tell whether it helps the CIO change the value his unit delivers. But if the examples of Freescale, Intel, McKesson, and others are any indication, the new mind-set should pay off for InfoInfinity.

Report on value for money forever

Like money, people, or anything else of value, IT is a scarce resource. Demonstrating value for money as we have described helps the CIO make the point that IT costs what it costs because a given level of service has a certain price—just as a Lexus sedan has a different price from a Subaru. Once the rest of the executive team understands that, there's room for meaningful discussions about which services matter most, and why. It is the beginning of effective business involvement in IT decision making.

It takes most IT organizations six to twelve months to design and implement an effective business-oriented measurement and reporting program—one that shows how well IT is doing in delivering the right services, at the right level of quality, at the right price. Whether or not the numbers look good, they give IT a good story to tell, because measuring is the essential first step in improving value and is recognized as such by every capable executive team.

Once under way, the program never stops. Value for money must be proved forever. It can never be taken for granted. We repeat: the need to show value for money in IT performance never goes away.

This doesn't mean that nothing changes in the conversation over time. When the measurement program begins, especially in an IT turnaround situation, most of IT's conversations with the rest of the business are about nothing except value for money. But as value for money is proved, those conversations occupy less time in monthly discussions with members of the executive team. According to Intel, once the IT benchmark reports started looking better, the senior team focused on other issues. When value for money is on the right track, executives need only be reminded that they are still getting the right services, at the right level of quality, for the right price, and that the CIO is working steadily to improve even more. They no longer need a lengthy conversation every month just to convince them that the money spent on IT is well managed.

"IT has gone from an opaque cost to an understood cost and value driver. The business is comfortable that we're measuring expense, quality, customer service—all the things you do to run a good business."[18]

—Randy Spratt, CIO, McKesson

Providing and proving value for money—becoming the "cheap information officer"—are the essential first steps in creating and demonstrating the business value of IT. By providing uncontested value for money, the CIO gets the credibility necessary to take the next step: working with the executive team to determine the investments in IT that will best improve business performance. This planning can be started as soon as the executive team is convinced that IT's value for money is improving substantially and will continue to improve, as demonstrated by a clear change in the tenor of conversations about IT's performance—for example, a shift in focus from "Why does IT cost so much?" to discussions centered on improving business outcomes. How to take that step is the topic of chapter 4.

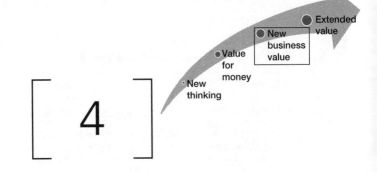

[4]

Master the Virtuous Cycle

An investment in knowledge always pays the best interest.

—Benjamin Franklin

L ET'S BEGIN THIS CHAPTER with a quiz. The reason will be apparent soon, we promise, and the results will be illuminating.

Using table 4-1 as a guide (see the next page), we'd like you to assess your organization's capabilities in the eighteen IT management tasks, ten of which are typically CIO responsibilities and eight of which are not. Use a scale from 1 to 10, where 1 = ineffective and 10 = highly effective. Ready? Go.

Finished? Great. Table 4-2 shows the way the scores averaged out for a survey of 153 senior executives conducted by MIT's CISR, using the same questionnaire and scoring guidelines.

Here's what makes the survey numbers important: of the eighteen common IT and non-IT tasks, *only four* (shown in bold type in table 4-2)—application development; BPR (business process redesign) and organizational change; needs identification; and IT oversight—have a statistically significant correlation to the business value provided by IT.[1] Enterprises that are better at

TABLE 4-1

Rate your company on these tasks

IT tasks	Business tasks
• Operations	• Funding
• Financial management	• Prioritizing
• Infrastructure/Architecture planning	• Relationship management
• Application development	• Strategic direction
• IT organization management	• Implementation support
• IT strategy	• Needs identification
• People management	• Using IT effectively
• Prioritizing	• IT oversight
• Relationship management	
• BPR/Organizational change	

any of the four provide higher business value in the eyes of the non-IT executives who benefit from that value.

All the other tasks are enablers and not value generators. They're about running IT and not about improving the business. In short, the most important business value comes not from managing the IT organization better, but from changing the business in valuable ways. (As we said in chapter 2, it's always about business performance.)

We cannot overemphasize the importance of this finding. Although effective CIOs do many IT tasks (such as operations,

TABLE 4-2

Survey results: How good is your enterprise at the key IT tasks?

IT tasks	Business tasks
• Operations (8.0)	• Funding (7.0)
• Financial management (6.7)	• Prioritizing (7.0)
• Infrastructure/architecture planning (6.5)	• Relationship management (6.9)
• **Application development (6.3)**	• Strategic direction (6.7)
• IT organization management (6.2)	• Implementation support (6.4)
• IT strategy (5.9)	• **Needs identification (6.3)**
• People management (5.8)	• Using IT effectively (5.8)
• Prioritizing (5.8)	• **IT oversight (5.5)**
• Relationship management (5.5)	
• **BPR/organizational change (5.5)**	

Source: Updated from George Westerman and Peter Weill, "What Makes an Effective CIO: The Perspective of Non-IT Executives," *MIT Sloan CISR Research Briefings* V(2C), July 2005.

infrastructure planning, IT organization management, and relationship management) better than their peers, those tasks have relatively little effect on business executives' perception of business value. There's no point in doing them much better than average. They provide only a foundation—of technology, skills, information, and, above all, credibility—on which CIOs and business executives can produce and harvest value. They are not value itself.

This means that to increase value from IT, you should not put all your effort into managing the IT organization; once you've established value for money, it's better to focus on identifying valuable business changes and getting a better return from every change.

The virtuous cycle is key to business value for IT

The four factors highlighted in table 4-2 constitute a *virtuous cycle* of IT investment activities (see figure 4-1).

- *Needs identification* is about finding opportunities to improve enterprise performance.

- *Business process redesign (BPR) and organizational change* means identifying how business processes must change to deliver higher levels of performance, and then ensuring that the organization changes its practices effectively.

- *Application development* involves designing, acquiring, installing, and testing technology solutions to implement process changes.

- *IT oversight* is about business leaders ensuring the IT unit is operating effectively and efficiently. Key elements of effective oversight are a *transparent investment process*, whose objective is to choose the most promising opportunities for investment in IT, and *measurement* (or harvesting), which is aimed at ensuring that investment decisions produce value by reinforcing accountability for the actions and changes that will deliver the value.

If your enterprise is like the enterprises whose survey responses are summarized in table 4-2, then you do needs identification and application development better than you do oversight and BPR/organizational change, and you don't do any of them especially well. The good news is that you can increase business value by incrementally improving *any* of the steps in the virtuous cycle. The better news is that because of the dependencies between these elements, you can achieve tremendous value by improving all these elements in concert. The value of needs identification increases when the enterprise uses BPR to shape needs into high-value opportunities. The value from application development is higher when BPR and needs identification are done well. The value of all investment increases when the enterprise knows clearly what it's hoping to obtain from change and it measures the desired outcomes.

FIGURE 4-1

Virtuous cycle of IT value

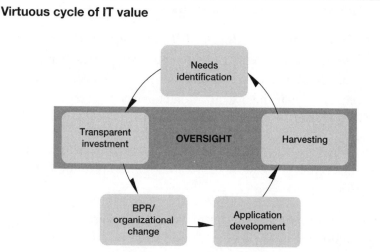

Source: Adapted from George Westerman and Peter Weill, "Getting Business Value from IT: The Non-IT Executive View," *MIT Sloan CISR Research Briefings*, V1(3A), December 2006.

The most important element is effective oversight. It's the glue that holds everything else together. And it turns all the tasks into a cycle of learning, and not something that repeats anew for each investment. Clarifying investment decisions and prioritization rules helps you get better at planning the value you will deliver, and it ensures that when you're identifying and implementing needs you also consider business changes as well as technology changes. This kind of clarity also provides the data needed to measure whether the project delivered the right returns. Measuring and communicating value ensure that the project was done effectively, and these activities help everyone improve planning and delivery processes. They also highlight opportunities for future change. Without oversight, the other tasks operate independently. With oversight, the tasks work together, and the team members learn each time the cycle spins.

That's what the virtuous cycle is, and that's why it matters. The rest of this chapter describes approaches to needs identification, the first part of the virtuous cycle. Chapter 5 continues the discussion by showing four ways to identify new sources of value for IT and align them with needs. Chapter 6 describes how to assess the value of opportunities and prioritize the resulting investment. Chapter 7 explains how CIOs can improve BPR, application development, and management of organizational change. Chapter 8 concludes our discussion of the virtuous cycle with a guide to measuring and harvesting benefits.

Start the virtuous cycle by understanding what matters

To show that IT improves business performance, you need to know which aspects of your business performance need improvement. That means understanding what matters most to the business. In many organizations, that's a nontrivial task. A typical business has many moving parts—and as many executives with varying personal interests and agendas. It can be difficult to figure out what matters most to whom, and not only for the CIO.

Often, the first way CIOs can improve business value is by helping their business counterparts clarify which types of value—which business outcomes—matter most. Then the executive team can use that focused view of value to make better decisions about which improvements are needed, which investments can help, and which steps can be taken to improve the value of every investment.

Focus is essential for successful investment in IT. Most enterprises use a comparable (if not the same) basic set of technologies for operating systems, languages, database management systems, business intelligence (BI), enterprise resource planning (ERP), customer relationship management (CRM), and other essential infrastructure or application requirements. It's not the technologies per se that differentiate an enterprise; it's the challenges and opportunities to which those technologies are applied that make the difference.

For example, CapitalOne, Wal-Mart, and Amazon.com are all heavy users of data mining, but each uses it differently, reflecting the strategic focus of the enterprise. At Amazon.com, data mining is used in support of customer intimacy (which books are you likely to enjoy, given the books you've purchased?). At CapitalOne, it is used in marketing (what types of products will appeal to ever-smaller segments of the market?). At Wal-Mart, it's about operational excellence for the supply chain (which products, in which sizes and containers, should be shipped to which stores by opening time tomorrow morning?).

"Too often, BI [business intelligence] technology is brought in as a solution looking for a problem. To a lot of people, it's intuitive that you need it. So you bring it in, and nothing happens, because it was envisioned through the wrong lens. If there's no true intellectual curiosity about customers, don't waste your money."[2]

—Butch Leonardson, CIO, Boeing Employees Credit Union

If the enterprise isn't focused, technologies like data mining might be applied to nothing in particular—with no particular outcomes to show for the investment. It's a classic example of the "IT delivers technology" value trap, especially because it's always done with the best of intentions.

Focus on what matters most

Your strategy is a good place to start looking for what matters most. But in many organizations, the strategy is unfocused or poorly understood, even by senior executives. If so, then analyzing your strategy may not be a viable approach to understanding what matters, and you'll need a different method to find the focus to identify the best candidate IT investments.

We suggest three ways to find the focus.

1. Clarify the strategy.

2. Analyze business processes.

3. Find the key operational metrics.

Each of these approaches has particular strengths and limitations. Not all will be useful for every company. But the CIO should use as many as possible, because the view offered by each approach illuminates opportunities or obstacles that aren't clear in the others.

Approach 1: Clarify the strategy

No business is ever proud to declare that it lacks a solid strategy. Most executives would agree that a well-defined and well-understood strategy helps all workers understand how their actions will improve enterprise performance—whether or not the executives in question think they have one themselves. Certainly CIOs working in enterprises that have a clear strategic focus are much more likely to be effective, in the sense that they know what to do next to move the business forward. Or we can state this principle from the opposite point of view: enterprises that understand how they compete, which is the role of strategy, are more likely to understand how they can use IT (as well as their other assets) to be more competitive.

The clear implication is that CIOs should do everything they can to help the executive team clarify the strategy. When the strategy is clear, it will also be clear how an IT organization that delivers value for money can deliver improved business performance.

Ask for the strategy

The most direct and obvious way to get your hands on the strategy is to ask your peers what their strategy is. On the other hand, if you have to ask, there's a good chance that it's not documented anywhere, and in that case there may be many different (and contradictory) versions of the strategy. In the CIO's favor is that she, like the CFO, has a legitimate reason to talk regularly to every executive and business unit head. By combining many views of unit-level strategies, the CIO can develop a larger picture of the strategy of the enterprise and of potential conflicts or lack of focus.

But this approach can be tricky. Successful serial CIO Bud Mathaisel puts it this way: "Timing is important. And usually the best time to have the longest-view conversations is when they are themselves in their own strategic planning mode. It's better than just walking into their office cold one day and saying, 'What are you thinking about the future? What should I be doing to help you in three years or four years or five years?' It's better when they themselves are in some sort of annual operating plan cycle or they're having a worldwide conference of their sales and materials executives and they're already wrapping their thinking around some form [of strategy]."[3]

Rather than ask for the strategy directly, it may be easier for the CIO to ask business executives questions about goals and obstacles. Here are some sample questions.

- What are the most important opportunities you see right now?

- What are the most important obstacles between you and those opportunities?

- What don't you know that you need to know to deal with the opportunities and obstacles?

- What can't you do that you need to do?

The CIO need not offer solutions; that can come later, when the messages have been absorbed. And be careful to follow Bud Mathaisel's advice not to ask too often. Ask at the right moment to get the information. Then, in other meetings, listen to the conversation to see what's changing. Asking questions to highlight an apparent change in strategy can be seen as a contribution. But repeatedly asking the same template of questions can be seen as a nuisance.

If you can't get the strategy by asking for it, find it another way

When you don't have the opportunity to ask about strategy, or when the answers you get are cloudy or contradictory, you need to look elsewhere. You can start at the enterprise level by examining public documents and statements. A few sources usually offer significant insight into management's strategy. Some of these are obvious, but we include them here for the sake of thoroughness.

- *What is discussed in the annual report?* Private sector businesses and many public agencies produce an annual report. This report—prepared for audiences that include regulators (legislators in the case of public agencies), shareholders (the public in the case of the agencies), and employees—describes the enterprise's recent history and plans. Statements made in the annual report are in effect publicly made promises, and CIOs can take them as seriously as any of the other audiences.[4]

- *What is discussed in the 10-K?* The Securities and Exchange Commission (SEC) requires that publicly traded companies file 10-K statements. They describe the company's strategy, its sources of competitive advantage, and risks as perceived by senior management. Executives can be sued for making false or misleading statements in the 10-K, so it can be considered a reliable source of information. But remember that the annual report and Form 10-K report only what the company wants to share (or is required to share). Many other aspects of strategy, performance, and risk are never shared with the outside world.

- *What have senior executives told investors and the press?* Most publicly traded companies hold regular conferences and meetings for investors. The statements made at these meetings are tracked by investors and investment advisers (sometimes as fodder for future shareholder lawsuits), so company executives do not make them lightly. Check the Web for any new releases, public statements, or analyst reports that mention future directions or commitments of the enterprise.

Next, move down a level or two in the organization. Examine current budget proposals for each business unit (including budget items that executives wanted but that were not approved this year). These documents show what business unit executives have seen fit to tell their bosses and the rest of the enterprise about their units' plans and performance. Also look at longer-term product road maps or other planning documents. Like any plans, these are subject to change, but they can help you understand the future goals and plans of the executives with whom you interact.

You can also use midlevel relationships to gain an understanding of strategy at the business unit level. Ask your application development heads to explain the strategies of their business unit counterparts. Poll your IT business unit relationship managers about what they're hearing from their counterparts. This is second-hand information, but it can be a valuable source of intelligence.

When all sources are exhausted, document what you believe the strategy to be, and play it back to the other members of the

"CIOs who say, 'We don't have a strategic plan in the business'—right! Do one! Suddenly you're a business leader. Lots of CIOs want a strategic business plan so they can do the IT plan. Go to the business leaders and get the plan going. Then you're a business leader."[5]

—Butch Leonardson, CIO, Boeing Employees Credit Union

executive team. They are sure to respond. They may confirm what you've written, or they may correct it. Either way, you'll know more than you did before about where the business thinks it's going.

Approach 2: Analyze business processes

Strategy is about plans. Business processes are about execution. Analysis of the business's processes provides a lot of important information about current and prospective capabilities that may be absent from the strategy. And if there's a gap between the capabilities of a business process and the strategy that depends on it, then you may have a significant opportunity for adding value via IT. Business unit leaders are certain to be interested in a discussion of their process; it's either their pride or the bane of their existence, and either way they'll want to talk about it.

The most important questions about processes are operational. What is the role of the process in the business? What are its capabilities in scale, cycle time, resource consumption, and quality? What are its vulnerabilities and associated risks? How does it relate to other processes? How does it compare to similar processes used by competitors? Can it accommodate prospective changes in the business that it supports?

Sam Coursen of Freescale Semiconductor uses the *value chain*—a well-known concept derived from Michael Porter's work on competitive strategy in the 1980s—and the processes that support it as the organizing principle for discussions of strategic needs.[6] The value chain concept is familiar to any MBA, and thus

FIGURE 4-2

Freescale Semiconductor value chain

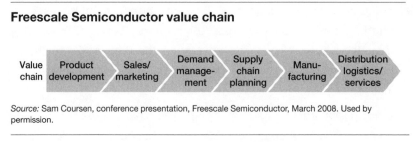

Source: Sam Coursen, conference presentation, Freescale Semiconductor, March 2008. Used by permission.

is a good way to discuss applications and business processes in terms that business executives understand. (Figure 4-2 depicts the value chain as it is conceived by Freescale.) Here are Coursen's words:

> Optimizing the cost and efficiency of IT processes is only half the [value] equation. The other half of the equation is everybody else's processes.
>
> Think of the value chain: we build products, we sell them, we fulfill the orders, we service after sale. That's how we add value. In IT, we've chunked Freescale up into twenty processes associated with that value chain. For each process we have an owner in the company. And we create a game plan for each process—supply chain, manufacturing, and so on: what's the current state, what are the opportunities to improve it, what's the future state? We get that locked in with the owner of the process.
>
> So instead of running around doing a thousand little fixes, which users can easily make you do—and none of the fixes have ROI!—we can focus on the big steps, like where do you want to be with the supply chain? Then the owner of the process is really on board with reengineering their process through strategic initiatives.
>
> Architecture is important here, but if you're talking about architecture in the sense of the technology, we don't even talk to the business about that. We talk to them at the level of the business process game plan. Then we translate that into the

underlying technical strategy and architecture. That technology architecture is an important strategy, but we don't engage the business on that unless they ask. But they don't ask. They don't get value out of the technical standards. They get value out of whether the business process improves.

Freescale's IT is pretty adamant that our IT strategy doesn't exist per se; it's the business domain strategy. We used to work with the power users in every function from the bottom up to develop the IT strategy, and it didn't necessarily connect to the business strategy. By coming from the top down, we were able to redirect IT effort on major initiatives. We shifted IT investments for supporting areas to the value chain of processes.[7]

Note a few things about Coursen's comments. First, his IT strategy is really the business domain strategy, so it is linked directly to the company's most important long-term priorities. Second, he develops the strategy process by process, working directly with process owners, and he's taken steps to ensure that ownership of processes is clear, so he's dealing with people who have the authority to make changes. Third, he doesn't discuss the technical architecture that supports strategy for a given process with the rest of the business unless he's asked—and he never is.

In short, where this discussion is concerned, it's really not about IT; it's all about business performance. And as this example shows, the CIO should never simply take the functional approach described by an executive—*how* the goals for the process are to be achieved—at face value as an accurate statement of what the executive really wants and needs. CIOs add lots of value by showing how technology can provide a better answer to that question.

Approach 3: Find the key operational metrics that managers are using

Many CIOs are focused on making the connection between IT performance and business financial performance, and they're frustrated by their inability to make a direct connection. The connection is much easier to make, and to measure, when it is framed in business operational metrics, which are leading indicators for financials. Operational metrics are also typically the metrics by which performance of a business process is measured, so they shed light on what managers believe matters most in the process.

For any given manager at any level of an enterprise, typically a small number of operational metrics drive the manager's decisions every day. Meaningful changes in business performance are expressed largely in terms of those metrics. If IT can help improve those metrics, then, by definition, the change will be perceived as valuable.

Questions that lead to those metrics include the following.

- *What metrics have an impact on the executive's compensation plan?* The executive compensation plan is often the most important driver for enterprise or business unit strategy. A CIO whose initiatives improve the metrics that an executive is measured on is more likely to win support (and avoid opposition) than one who doesn't.

- *What key operational metrics do managers track every day? What do these metrics tell those managers?* At Career Education Corporation, one of the leading players in the adult education industry, the status of student loans and classroom attendance are watched very carefully as critical leading indicators for revenues. A drop in either metric might signal imminent departure of the students involved.

- *What are current levels of performance for these metrics?* It was a major breakthrough for the Career Education Corporation when IT began to deliver enrollment, attendance, and loan status numbers in real time, as opposed to the weekly and monthly reports to which management had grown accustomed. Faster delivery of these leading indicators made it possible for managers to spot and handle risky situations before they developed into emergencies.

- *Are these metrics consistent with the strategy?* In other words, are managers emphasizing the performance that is most consistent with the requirements of the formal strategy? A common conflict arises when the performance goals contained in the executive compensation plan are not aligned with the company's formal strategy. In many cases, if not most, conflicts are resolved in favor of increased executive compensation. In other words, the executive compensation plan usually defines the real strategy.

- *What key operational metrics are reported to suppliers, customers, investors, or regulators?* What do these metrics tell them? What decisions do these external parties make based on those metrics?

Gartner's Business Value Framework, created by Gartner analysts Michael Smith and Audrey Apfel based on industry sources such as the Supply Chain Council, represents some of the most widely used operational metrics worldwide.[8] This framework, which can be a useful source of operational metrics, is depicted in table 4-3.

Operational metrics and outcomes matter
for noncommercial enterprises, too.

Understanding business operational metrics and the outcomes they represent is as important for nonprofits and governmental agencies as it is for commercial enterprises. Consider Campus Crusade for Christ, an evangelical Christian organization that maintains a substantial presence on college campuses across the United States. The organization's services include telephone help lines for students seeking counsel for spiritual or emotional crises.

The organization's CIO, Trey Lewis, was having trouble conveying the value of IT's services to the organization. He realized that part of the problem was the measures he was using, such as network uptime and total cost of ownership for IT assets. These metrics mattered to him and his team but meant nothing to the executives who paid for and benefited from IT's services.

TABLE 4-3

The Gartner Business Value Framework

Business aspect	Aggregates	Primes			
Demand management	Market responsiveness	Target market index	Market coverage index	Market share index	Opportunity/threat index
		Product portfolio index	Channel profitability index	Configure-ability index	
	Sales effectiveness	Sales opportunity index	Sales cycle index	Sales close index	Sales price index
		Cost of sales index	Forecast accuracy	Customer retention index	
	Product development effectiveness	New products index	Feature function index	Time to market index	R&D success index
Supply management	Customer responsiveness	On-time delivery	Order fill rate	Material quality	Service accuracy
		Service performance	Customer care performance	Agreement effectiveness	Transformation ratio
	Supplier effectiveness	Supplier on-time delivery	Supplier order fill rate	Supplier material quality	Supplier service accuracy
		Supplier service performance	Supplier care performance	Supplier agreement effectiveness	Supplier transformation ratio
	Operational efficiency	Cash to cash cycle time	Conversion cost	Asset utilization	Sigma value
Support services	Human resources responsiveness	Recruitment effectiveness index	Benefits administration index	Skills inventory index	Employee training index
		HR advisory index	HR total cost index		
	Information technology responsiveness	Systems performance	IT support performance	Partnership ratio	Service level effectiveness
		New projects index	IT total cost index		
	Finance & regulatory responsiveness	Compliance index	Accuracy index	Advisory index	Cost of service index

Source: M. Smith and A. Apfel, "The Gartner Business Value Model: A Framework for Measuring Business Performance," Gartner Research Note G00139413, May 31, 2006.

In an effort to link his performance to metrics that mattered to the organization, he began to emphasize instead IT's contribution to the organization's ability to serve the spiritual and emotional needs of students and win converts. He considered metrics such as the following:

- The volume of calls fielded by the organization, including trends over time; average IT and organizational cost per call and convert

- Wait times for help lines during peak and nonpeak times; hang ups of waiting callers during those times

- IT's ability to support expansion of the organization to new campuses, including costs and cycle time for establishing new offices

- Effectiveness and usage of IT-supported channels, such as Web sites and chat rooms, in supporting communications with students; percentage of users of those channels who join or contribute to the organization

These measures and others served two purposes for Lewis. First, he was able to link his unit's performance more directly to measures that mattered to the senior executive team. Second, he helped the senior executive team develop a stronger set of metrics they could use to manage their own units. In other words, focusing on the metrics that mattered to the enterprise served as the basis for a discussion about how information technologies and people could most effectively help the organization achieve and expand on its mission—and this is where the value is.

Less than a year later, Lewis felt he was in a very different position. His unit was valued more by the rest of the business, and he assumed leadership of a new channel strategy aimed at building online communities. Executives began calling him to ask for IT's help in improving their units' performance, and he was included in periodic sessions that considered the current and long-term strategy of the organization.[9]

Use what you've learned
to develop opportunities

At this point, you have gathered information that includes the following:

- The best available description of the company's strategies

- A high-level analysis of the company's processes

- The operational metrics that are most important to business leaders at multiple levels

The company's strategies tell you where the business wants to go. The analysis of the company's processes tells you whether the current processes can take it there. The operational metrics tell you how improvements in performance will be measured.

This is the essential information you need to generate insight into opportunities for investment. *An opportunity exists when a process can or must be improved to advance the strategy and when it is clear how the improvements will affect business performance in observable, measurable terms.* Some executives inside and outside IT have internalized this knowledge to the point that valuable opportunities present themselves as inspirations, as in the example of Gonpo Tsering, senior executive vice president and member of the executive board of DKSH, whose case is described in chapter 5. For others, formal, structured approaches may be useful—for example, systematically linking strategies to processes and processes to performance metrics, then analyzing in detail the set of options to move performance to a higher level. This is the approach that a management consulting company would take. Whether your preferred approach is closer to one of these extremes or falls between them, the common element is familiarity with the company's strategies and operations.

From the point of view of needs identification, the next step is to generate and rank proposals for seizing the opportunities. That's the subject of our next two chapters.

$$\begin{bmatrix} 5 \end{bmatrix}$$

Find the Sources
of New Value

A T ROOT, IT organizations have two basic levers at their disposal for creating value. They can improve decision making by improving information quality or timeliness, or they can increase efficiency, quality, and functionality by improving processes.

By adding a dimension that represents the reach of the mechanisms by which information or automation is provided—the scope of the audience, inside and outside the enterprise, that is touched in some way by IT-supported change—we produce figure 5-1, which represents the full range of approaches IT can apply to improve business differentiation and competitiveness.

In any business, the IT organization might have opportunities to make important contributions to business performance in more than one of these ways. In fact, we often see that initiatives beginning in one quadrant enable others as improvements in information and processes create a stable, highly functional platform for further change.

For example, DKSH is the world's leading market expansion services provider, with $8 billion in sales in 2008. The company is based in Switzerland but has focused on Asia for almost 150 years.

FIGURE 5-1

Four sources of new value from IT

IT can improve business performance in four ways, and all are high value.

	Internal informing Provide information to improve operational decisions.	**External informing** Embed information into products and services.
Improve decision making		
Improve process	**Optimizing** Improve or transform internal processes through technology.	**Reshaping** Change how customers and partners interact with the enterprise and its products/services.

Source of value (left label)

Internal	External

Scope of change

DKSH has four business units—Consumer Goods, Healthcare, Performance Materials, and Technology—through which it offers sourcing, sales, marketing, distribution, and logistics services. In 2005 the company implemented new distribution center processes and technology supported by SAP systems, an optimization initiative aimed at the company's operational performance as a logistics provider. Soon afterward, senior executive VP of operations and business support Gonpo Tsering realized that the company's new IT platform and global scope provided it with proprietary regional sales information that was of great value to customers. DKSH could apply external informing to offer customers summarized sales and market trend information along with its shipping services. For example, it could tell a mom-and-pop corner store retailer in Shanghai that he should order a particular brand of chewing gum, because sales of the brand were increasing steadily and moving up the coast of China on a trend line that would take it to Shanghai in a matter of weeks. DKSH became in effect a supplier of business intelligence to its customers as well as a logistics company, increasing the company's

The four sources model: How IT improves business performance

- *Optimizing:* Processes internal to the company are improved or transformed through automation. Though optimizing is typically about incremental process improvements, it can also include actions that replace whole sets of applications and processes.

- *Reshaping:* Automation is used to change how customers and partners interact with the enterprise, how they work with the enterprise's products and services, or the levels and kinds of service provided. These may be large, such as integrating the global supply chain, or smaller, such as providing customers with self-service features they formerly had to request through a salesperson or call center.

- *Internal informing:* Information is supplied to internal audiences to support decision making related to specific operational issues. Resulting performance improvements may be visible to external parties such as customers and suppliers, but the information itself typically is not.

- *External informing:* Information is supplied directly to external parties, such as customers and suppliers, to enhance or change the enterprise's value proposition, relationships, or operations.

value proposition to customers large and small and changing its strategic positioning.[1]

Similarly, Career Education Corporation, the fastest-growing company in the adult education industry, conducted an optimization initiative in 2001 to replace dozens of administrative systems—the legacy of a growth-by-acquisition strategy—with a single consolidated system. The information available from the consolidated system created internal and external informing opportunities: to dramatically improve the speed and accuracy of managerial decision making about class enrollments, attendance, and student loans, to better target profitable locations for new schools, and to provide enrollees and students with up-to-date information about courses, grades, and loans.[2]

When opportunities are identified, explore the sources of new IT value

Although much of the effort of your IT unit is spent meeting requests from the various stakeholders in your enterprise, simply taking orders is a value trap. CIOs who provide high value to their enterprises do more than take orders. They help shape stakeholder requests into forms that are more valuable for the enterprise. And they suggest new initiatives that provide value well beyond what the other stakeholders can suggest.

Once you have identified strategic issues and opportunities, as described in chapter 4, you are in a position to shape new initiatives. The *four sources model* is a useful framework for this purpose.

Let's look at each of the four sources of new IT value in turn.

Optimizing

Optimizing opportunities revolve around using IT to streamline processes through automation or consolidation. For example, at Intel, maintenance technicians had to move from machinery to a green screen and back again while doing their work. Intel's IT team developed a single handheld device to reduce the time and effort involved in this maintenance. The mobile device combined numerous green screen applications on a single mobile interface, streamlining the workflow for technicians and improving equipment uptime. Other optimizing opportunities may exist in automating manual processes (or process steps), eliminating steps in a process, providing automated help for manual tasks, or replacing multiple legacy systems with a new streamlined platform.

To explore optimizing opportunities, ask these questions:

- What are the processes that contribute to the key operational performance metrics for the enterprise?

- What are the major steps in those processes? Who are the key personnel and functions involved in each of those steps?

- How do cycle times and efficiency measures for those processes compare with similar processes elsewhere in the enterprise or in other enterprises?

- What are the most important obstacles those personnel face?

- Can we automate one or more specific capabilities for those personnel that will reduce or eliminate one or more of those obstacles?

- Can we improve the process by eliminating process steps or making process steps easier?

- Given the enterprise's goals for growth in revenues or profits and the implied performance requirements, what new capabilities could we introduce to the enterprise by improving or consolidating existing information systems and business processes?

The people best placed to ask and answer these questions are the personnel involved in a process and the IT personnel who directly support them. Indeed, one sure way to generate optimizing ideas is to embed IT personnel physically in the business units they support.

Reshaping

Reshaping opportunities improve business performance by changing the way customers and suppliers interact with the enterprise and its products or services. Reshaping may include reducing costs by off-loading internal processes to external parties, such as offering customers a self-service capability. Other reshaping activities include making process interactions easier across the enterprise's boundaries; making it easier for customers to work with the enterprise; or supporting the enterprise in working with other enterprises. Wal-Mart's supply chain initiatives, for example, make Wal-Mart's processes more efficient by requiring suppliers to use standard processes.

To identify reshaping opportunities, ask these questions:

- What are the pain points in the way our processes work with parties outside the enterprise?

- How can we make it easier to do business with the enterprise?

- How can we improve our processes by changing the way we work with external parties?

- How can we make ourselves more valuable to those other parties by improving *their* processes?

- Consistent with the broad strategic objectives and performance requirements of the enterprise, what new ways can we use to get customers or partners more engaged in working with our enterprise?

Many reshaping opportunities are identified in a similar way to optimizing opportunities but involve external as well as internal stakeholders. Especially in business process outsourcing relationships and other high-level partnerships, IT plays an important role in the customer's operations, and the CIO works closely with customers. Bud Mathaisel, in his role as CIO and chief process officer at Solectron, dedicated a percentage of his time to meet with customers and suppliers so they could improve collaboration. Ideas come from any source, in fact, that sheds light on how the business and its customers engage, including business analysts, relationship managers, customer service specialists, business unit and enterprise executives, or customers and suppliers themselves.

Like optimization, reshaping often involves extensive business process reengineering. It can be more difficult than optimization, however, when it involves changing processes that are shared with multiple organizations.

Internal informing

Internal informing opportunities arise when IT provides information that enterprise employees can use to improve their own performance. The Boston Red Sox credit an innovative application of information to hiring and coaching decisions with helping the professional baseball club win its first World Series in eighty-six years. CapitalOne places information in the hands of its marketing personnel, along with easy-to-use tools, so that they can conduct thousands of experiments each year selling new credit products to various customer segments.

As the examples show, internal informing isn't about blindly firing information at the enterprise in the hopes that someone will be able to use it. Rather, it's about identifying who will use specific information for a specific purpose with a specific outcome. To identify opportunities for internal informing, ask these questions.

- What do specific executives or roles in our organization— names or titles—want to know that they don't know now?

- What questions will those people answer when they get the information?

- What actions will they take when the questions are answered?

- What changes in capabilities and outcomes will result?

  - Will cycle times for key decisions change, with impacts on costs, risks, or revenues?

  - Will errors be reduced or quality otherwise enhanced?

- Will customers perceive a difference in responsiveness or quality?

- Will investment decisions be more accurate, producing increased yields or lower risks?

- Will some other observable outcome result?

- What information does our enterprise gather that is not used well by other processes? What other processes could use that knowledge?

- Which processes rely on standard operating procedure (SOP) or intuitive judgments when better decisions could be made with better information?

- Which processes that use dated or unintegrated data could be improved with real-time, integrated information?

Questions such as these are often best answered by the executives in charge of particular business units and (as always) by the IT relationship managers assigned to the business unit. In many cases, executives also have people on their staffs whose responsibility is to know and understand the numbers that are driving the business. Those staff members may not have exalted titles, but often they wield significant influence as trusted advisers. We have seen cases in which such personnel, when asked about the value of a particular piece of information, instantly recited a hard dollar estimate supported by a detailed and accurate rationale.

"A lot of us have learned that if you try to work forwards from the technology, you get a lot of failures. But if you start with the decisions, and talk about what information, with what timing, is essential, it works."[3]

—Guido Sacchi, CEO, Moneta Corporation (former CIO, CompuCredit)

External informing

External informing is a powerful source of value that few firms have found ways to harness. By providing customers and suppliers with information that other enterprises cannot provide, you cement tighter relationships with those external parties, providing value that goes well beyond the products and services they buy. Here are examples:

- Progressive Insurance provides information on competitors' prices as well as its own, helping customers feel more confident when selecting Progressive as an insurer.

- Consumer packaged goods enterprises such as Procter & Gamble provide retailers with sales data by stock keeping unit (SKU), allowing them to better understand purchasing patterns in their stores.

- Auto manufacturers provide information about future products and production plans to their networks of suppliers, allowing suppliers to bid on new work, suggest new component designs, or adjust their own product plans.

- When an IT security incident affects a Symantec customer, the company notifies other customers running similar software that they may have a vulnerability.

- Financial services companies provide customers with information on their overall portfolios as well as the performance of products they do not own, allowing customers to understand how their portfolio performance matches benchmarks and how they can adjust their assets appropriately.

To identify opportunities for *external informing*, ask these questions:

- What are the outcomes that customers seek when they use our (or competitors') products and services?

- What outcomes do partners or other external stakeholders seek when dealing with us?

- What does the customer or partner need to know to get that outcome? Do we, or anyone else, supply that information? If not, can we?

- What information do we already have that others would consider valuable for their decision making?

- Can we embed information directly into our product as a functional capability or a decision aid? Can we provide it through our value network?

As with reshaping opportunities, questions such as these might be answered by a wide range of personnel, from customers themselves to anyone in the enterprise whose role involves frequent contact with customers and other external stakeholders.

No matter where an idea comes from, it must be analyzed further to determine its impact on business performance, both in operational improvements and in the impact on profit and loss (P&L). In chapter 6 we discuss assessment of investment opportunities in more detail.

No single approach is the right one for all enterprises at all times

The four sources of IT value do not represent a maturity model, in which the highest level is presumed to be the most desirable. None of these approaches is intrinsically of higher value than the others. External initiatives are not somehow better because they move beyond the boundaries of the enterprise. And decision-making improvements are not superior to process improvements just because the former often helps managers instead of lower-level employees. Any of the four approaches to adding value via

IT might be the right one for a specific enterprise at a specific time. Furthermore, an initiative in one quadrant can be the foundation for many opportunities in the same or different quadrants.

CIOs should strive to help the business get the focus it needs to use the right approach, keeping in mind that the CIO in most cases will serve as an agent of change and not the sponsor. We have selected several cases involving CIOs who work in such focused businesses, each of which illustrates one or more of the four approaches to delivering value via IT.

- *Optimizing:* Broadcom's executive team wants its IT to be "like air"—the unseen environment that makes everything else work. Accordingly, Broadcom's IT team focuses tactically on removing obstacles to effective performance for Broadcom's engineers and designers so that they can work faster and more effectively to bring exciting products to market more quickly than competitors.

- *Internal informing:* Sharp Healthcare uses information to assist clinical workers in diagnosis and treatment, improving quality and cost of service through information dynamics.

- *Reshaping*: LFSCo (a pseudonym for a large financial services company) powers growth by continuously extending and improving the way customers use its services.

- *External informing:* DKSH uses IT strategically, embedding information of critical importance to its customers in its offerings as a way to differentiate its services from those of its competitors in the Asia-Pacific region.

These companies, and the ways they have used IT to increase competitive differentiation, are illustrated in figure 5-2. Although each serves as an example of one of the four quadrants, you'll notice in their stories that each success led to additional opportunities in another quadrant. The ability to deliver more value

FIGURE 5-2

Use IT to deliver the right value for the enterprise

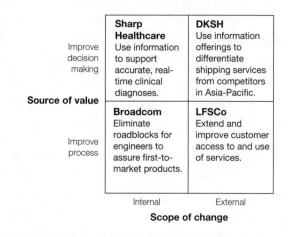

		Internal	External
Source of value	Improve decision making	**Sharp Healthcare** Use information to support accurate, real-time clinical diagnoses.	**DKSH** Use information offerings to differentiate shipping services from competitors in Asia-Pacific.
	Improve process	**Broadcom** Eliminate roadblocks for engineers to assure first-to-market products.	**LFSCo** Extend and improve customer access to and use of services.

Scope of change

comes from the trust and credibility built by delivering on prior value. The stories behind these companies and their CIOs follow.

Broadcom: Optimizing makes IT "like air"

Broadcom, founded in 1991, is one of the largest fabless semiconductor companies in the world, creating chips and software for wired and wireless communications. Its customers include Cisco, Nortel, and Motorola, and the company's market leadership discipline is product development. The company had sales of $3.67 billion at the end of 2006, when we first spoke to senior VP and CIO Ken Venner; sales grew to $4.66 billion in 2008.

Broadcom is an example of how IT can improve business performance and competitiveness dramatically, even when the technology or information delivered by the IT team is not an explicit component of the company's products or services. What makes IT a competitive weapon for Broadcom is a clear understanding by everyone of exactly how the company competes: via rapid development of outstanding products using superior partnerships.

Ken Venner came to the company as a turnaround CIO in 2000. Initially Venner focused on fixing IT's performance—delivering value for money. "First, I hired really great, really smart people," says Venner. "I focused on enabling the [internal Broadcom] customer to do what they need to do. I put the IT people in with their customers. We defined the 80 percent of the routine stuff that IT people do as processes, so we could minimize the time and effort. And then we marketed it all like crazy, so people knew what we were doing and wanted to engage us."[4]

With value for money coming into focus, Venner looked for opportunities to optimize performance for the engineers who create Broadcom's products. "What differentiates us [IT] is that we highly tune our environment for our engineering community," says Venner. "We deliver all the infrastructure and tools that they use for product design, delivery, and supply chain functionality. Our applications deeply focus on how our engineers work seamlessly around the world. The heads of engineering and I look at blocks of engineering effort, aiming to reduce the time from concept to finished product." Measurement of IT's contribution to this metric is not precise: "I know we've increased our first-to-market performance, but we have not correlated that to IT spend." Nevertheless, reductions in overall product development cycle time clearly benefit from IT's contribution, and management sees the investment in those terms.

Optimizing was not the only avenue to business value for Broadcom IT. Broadcom advances its market share through strategic partnerships with the top two or three original equipment manufacturers in attractive industry segments. Partnerships are improved by internal optimizing activities as well as by specific reshaping approaches. Broadcom's initiatives as of 2006 included a supply chain collaboration with a large customer that required business process and IT changes. Value was framed in two ways: gaining access to a strategic market via the customer, and gaining new revenues from that customer. "The business immediately saw the opportunity for this large customer to become part of our supply chain ecosystem," says Venner.

Broadcom's IT value at a glance

- *Key business outcomes:* High product quality, rapid product development and time to market, strong relationships with key OEMs

- *IT focus: Optimization to* remove tactical obstacles to engineering staff and reshaping to enable strategic partnerships

"Responsibility for delivering the benefits was shared between the business and IT."

He adds, "Being able to play with numbers one, two, and three in any market is a potent metric for our entire executive team. It means having the highest quality and the fastest time to market. Our potential partners ask us for core IT capabilities around collaborative communication and supply chain management."

FIGURE 5-3

Broadcom's sources of IT value

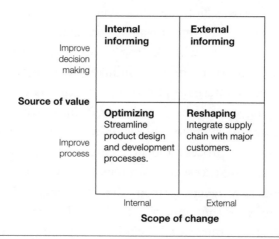

Those core capabilities create the environment in which IT is like air. Figure 5-3 shows how Broadcom's IT strategy fits into the value quadrant.

Sharp HealthCare: Internal informing, built on enterprise optimizing

Sharp is the leading health care provider in San Diego, California. In 2007 it won the prestigious Malcolm Baldrige National Quality Award, and the award committee cited Sharp's IT as a contributor to the award.[5]

Sharp, funded in part via philanthropy, is a not-for-profit enterprise with fourteen thousand employees, seven hospitals, three affiliated medical groups, and a health plan offering. According to Bill Spooner, senior VP and CIO, "Our basic theme is to improve patient satisfaction by improving physician and employee satisfaction. Our key 'pillars of value' are finance, service, quality, people (employees), growth, and community. When patients walk away feeling they've been taken care of, we believe growth, finance, and community will take care of themselves."[6]

In addition to its recent Baldridge award, Sharp's Web site has won numerous awards, and Sharp is one of six health care systems in the United States to be on the "most wired" award list for all the years of this Hospitals & Health Networks award. But Sharp's IT budget is not aggressive. "Since the late 1990s, we had pursued a best-of-breed strategy for our IT applications," says Spooner. "There were no alternatives. No vendor could do most of the critical functions. But our integration of the multiple applications was not effective. Physicians still had to go to multiple systems to get their data," a situation that does not contribute to efficient and effective health care.

In a highly strategic optimizing project, Sharp replaced its polyglot information systems environment with an integrated product suite, which it called the Core Patient Care Project. The desired outcomes of the project include better patient care, a better working environment for physicians and nurses, and modernization of the hospital facility to meet the California seismic law requiring buildings to withstand earthquakes. The consolidation improved internal processes significantly, as noted by the Baldridge award. But it also provided additional opportunities for value.

One capability of the Core Patient Care Project illustrates how Sharp uses information to improve physician decision making. Diagnosis is one of the most important steps in treatment. Generally, a correct diagnosis early in treatment leads to better outcomes for the patient and lower costs for treatment; an incorrect diagnosis tends to produce poor outcomes and high costs. Physicians vary in their diagnostic abilities, and any physician can produce diagnoses of varying quality depending on a variety of personal and situational factors such as the physician's mood, fatigue, knowledge and memory, familiarity with the conditions presented by the patient, the patient's manner and appearance, and so on.

Computers have no such human frailties. When presented with a list of symptoms and measurements, a computer compares the data to an encyclopedic body of knowledge, responding with the same range of possible diagnoses every time. By augmenting

---

Sharp's IT value at a glance

- *Key business outcomes:* Improve patient satisfaction by improving physician and employee satisfaction and capabilities; "six pillars" of value: finance, service, quality, people (employees), growth, and community

- *IT focus:* Integrate hospital processes and information systems to optimize efficiency and effectiveness of health care personnel; internal informing to maximize quality of health care decision making

FIGURE 5-4

Sharp's sources of IT value

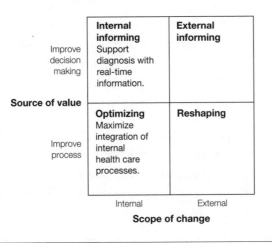

human judgment with machine judgment—internal informing for physicians—Sharp dramatically improves the consistency and quality of diagnoses, and so outcomes and costs. Figure 5-4 shows how Sharp's IT strategy fits into the value quadrants.

LFSCo: Continuous reshaping via IT

IT's most visible value for LFSCo comes from reshaping customer processes for credit processing. "We add value to merchants in four ways," says the CIO. "First, we make the POS [point of sale equipment] always available in the merchant's store whenever a customer comes in to use it. Second, we mitigate merchants' risk. Lots of cash in a store makes a merchant a target, and checks are a risk. Third, merchants can anticipate being paid within thirty days with us—even within forty-eight hours if they need it. Fourth, our new products attract more people into their store, and the merchants get paid when someone uses the POS in their store."[7]

LFSCo's IT value at a glance

- *Key business outcomes:* Use of POS to deliver reliable service and increasing range of products and services to merchants and their customers; use of technology infrastructure and applications to beat competitors to market with new products and services

- *IT focus:* Continuous, reliable IT operations; continuous reduction in cost per business transaction, ensuring greater margins while IT supports rapid business growth; continuously increasing IT productivity to reduce time to market and cost for innovative products and services

But IT cannot deliver value only through external activities. Continuous optimizing is also essential. Even here, in this fast-growing financial services company whose management sees IT capability as a competitive weapon, management pays strict attention to cost-effective operations. The company expects the IT cost per business transaction to decline, even as absolute IT costs rise.

IT budget conversations have three dimensions: (1) investments in IT needed to support new products or services; (2) increases in IT capacity needed to support organic business growth; and (3) tools to make the IT organization more productive—for example, a new programming tool. In a company whose IT-related costs are 25 percent of the overall budget, improvements in IT productivity have a direct impact on IT costs per business transaction. Because delivery of new products and services is done via the POS network, IT productivity also has a direct impact on time to market. Says the CIO:

We're growing faster than our competitors, in part because we deploy technology more aggressively. We are launching a new product where people can go into a store or restaurant and

FIGURE 5-5

LFSCo's sources of IT value

	Internal informing	External informing
Improve decision making		
Source of value		
Improve process	**Optimizing** Maximize efficiency and cost-effectiveness of IT.	**Reshaping** Change merchant and consumer behaviors toward POS network.
	Internal	External

Scope of change

pay their bills, as if they were in a bank, using their debit card at our POS terminal. In addition, ninety million prepaid cell phone owners can recharge their cell phone minutes using an LFSCo POS. Our competitors can't do that.

IT contributes directly to our ability to compete. We get questions about costs with new initiatives, not about value. They ask us, "Can you do it faster, more cheaply?" No one ever says, "Don't do it."

Figure 5-5 shows how LFSCo's IT strategy fits into the value quadrants.

DKSH: Putting information into the value proposition

Market expansion services provider DKSH is an example of an apparently growing trend: the business executive whose vision for the enterprise involves plenty of excellent IT. In such cases, the expectation of high value from IT is already present, and the CIO need only deliver it. This is what appealed to Dieter Schlosser when he joined DKSH as VP IT from DaimlerChrysler in 2005. "It was very exciting to see how committed DKSH top management is to IT. My boss [hires only] top people in IT . . . and that sets the tone in the organization for this journey."[8]

As noted earlier, in 2005 senior executive VP Gonpo Tsering decided to standardize business operations and create a shared services center, an initiative supported by a global rollout of SAP's enterprise resource planning software. Tsering's executive colleagues were initially skeptical of this optimizing initiative. The business was growing profitably, and most colleagues anticipated more risk than reward from such major change. Tsering realized that he needed to focus on more than cost. "I told our CEO that by centralizing IT, I could probably save 33 percent, maybe more," says Tsering. "But that's not what it's about. It's about risk management, competitive advantage, standardization and harmonization, agility of the business model, and taking waste out of the current processes."

It helped that the senior executive VP, and not an IT executive, was pitching this change. "I had to convince them that a tube of toothpaste and a luxury watch are essentially the same in terms of business process," says Tsering. "This was a paradigm shift, but I convinced the CEO in about eight minutes, and together we convinced the chairman in about an hour." The winning argument was based on risks to current services and future growth rather than on costs of current operations.

In our interviews, Tsering and Schlosser emphasized the fact that DKSH, being in a services business, could not operate without its IT. "If we had no IT for more than one day, we'd be out of business," Tsering says. Consolidating and standardizing infrastructure could go a long way in reducing availability risk. But more was at stake. The two men focused also on standardizing business processes and applications to reduce risks to accuracy and agility faced by the growing business.[9] According to Schlosser, this argument was convincing. "The board believed that our growth targets could only be achieved with standard processes and IT. We wanted to duplicate what we were doing in our top countries, to offer the same level of services across Asia. IT was our instant vehicle to do that, and our enabler for supporting the business in the future."

In addition to the operational benefits of optimizing, a major source of value was internal and external informing, achieved via a real-time data warehouse that Schlosser and his staff built on top of the shared services engine. According to Schlosser, "I thought we had to streamline the information flow. Soon I realized I was on the wrong track. We had to streamline and make it more efficient, but we had to build it up!" Tsering adds:

> You don't do distribution for ten to twenty years for the same supplier. You're constantly renegotiating contracts and outsourcing deals. Moving the boxes is a commodity. Everyone can do that, though of course you have to be high quality, manage inventory, take care of lost sales, and so on. The added value is information. Consumer behavior and market information is very compelling. For example, in China, we have a branch structure, and we have dedicated sales teams related to geographies. With the information that we keep in SAP, and knowing which teams work in which geography, we can give behavioral reports out that describe the market, the consumer behavior, the points of sales. Many of the principals [large trading partners] can't generate this kind of information on their own.
>
> With the information factory, we provide three things. First, market information—what's selling, where. Second, for companies that don't want to do their own information warehouses, we give them access to our business warehouse. Finally, for companies that want analytical tools, we offer access to the analytical tools in the business warehouse. We offer one thousand different reports in Malaysia alone, and one hundred fifty thousand throughout Asia on a daily basis.

FIGURE 5-6

DKSH's sources of IT value

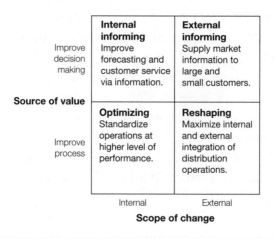

Tsering says, "If you have world-class, totally documented certified processes in place, with reports at the tip of your finger, plus market information, this is really powerful. We collect this information but haven't used it in the past. Now we can use it." According to DKSH, their implementation of SAP's "business warehouse" information management toolset is the second largest in the world. Figure 5-6 shows how DKSH's IT strategy fits into the four value quadrants.

When you've identified ideas aimed at specific needs, the next step in the virtuous cycle is transparent investment—assessment and selection of investment proposals using clearly defined criteria. That's the subject of our next chapter.

DKSH's IT value at a glance

- *Key business outcomes:* Standardized excellence in logistics operations throughout the company; high value-add to customers based on access to market information

- *IT focus:* Automation of the enterprise to achieve high quality and efficiency of scale; use of information generated from operations to offer market reporting and analysis services to customers

$$\begin{bmatrix} 6 \end{bmatrix}$$

Assess and Select
IT Investments Transparently

C HAPTERS 4 and 5 discussed the first part of the virtuous cycle: needs identification. In this chapter we turn our attention to the next step, transparent investment. In a transparent investment process, opportunities meet a well-defined prioritization process designed to identify winning proposals. The output of the process is a set of approved initiatives for development (along with a list of rejected or deferred initiatives).

It goes without saying that choosing the right projects is as important to delivering value as strong execution in project management. In IT, as in finance, not all opportunities are equal, and the resources available for investment are scarce. Choices must be made in every enterprise. The only question is how to choose. There are two ways to make these decisions. The first is to use a transparent process and clear criteria for assessment, and the second is anything else.

"Anything else" includes basing your decision on politics, intuition, or a host of other less-rigorous approaches. Some of these approaches work more or less acceptably for some companies. Some entrepreneurial leaders, such as Steve Jobs and Richard Branson, have a legendary ability to identify big bets that will pay off. Most people don't. Over time, the organizations that produce the highest yields from their investments tend to be the ones with solid methods practiced systematically. Certainly that's how Warren Buffett does it. It's also how the successful CIOs we've studied do it.

At a very basic level, successful assessment processes share certain characteristics. They are structured and transparent. They work in a certain way every time, and the structure is well understood by everyone involved, from the parties who submit proposals to the decision makers. Even the exception processes are transparent to all. The basics of the process involve project sponsors (1) developing a formal proposal that incorporates estimated benefits, risks, and resource requirements and (2) submitting the proposal to decision makers who select preferred investments from the proposals.

In more advanced enterprises, proposals define benefits in specific operational or financial business performance categories, which are weighted in terms of importance to the investment decision. Using specific categories ensures that proposals can be compared apples to apples, and it allows project sponsors to readily understand how to adjust initiatives to deliver a more attractive mix of benefits and risks. Proposals are ranked by decision makers—perhaps a single senior executive but more often a committee—using the weighted criteria, with adjustments allowed for a range of specified reasons. In effective processes, proposals that rank highest on the weighted criteria tend to rise near to the top of the approved list.

At Intel, project sponsors commit to making improvements on one or more operational performance metrics or "value dials" (see table 6-1). Each click of a value dial has a specific financial value, as assessed by Intel's internal finance staff. Focusing on value dials allows managers to concentrate on measurements that can be readily assessed, and avoids difficulties that arise when managers can attach their own dollar estimates to project benefits.[1]

In short, effective prioritization mechanisms are defined in terms of responsibilities, process, and criteria for decision making. Because the process is defined, it can be improved, meaning that

TABLE 6-1

Intel IT sets benchmarks and measures returns in multiple business performance categories.

- Days of inventory
- Days of receivables
- Head count reduction
- Head count productivity
- Head count turnover
- Materials discounts
- Capital hardware and software avoidance
- Unit and other cost avoidance

- Factory uptime
- Scrap reduction
- Risk avoidance
- Time to market
- Open new markets
- Optimize existing markets
- Cross-selling
- Vendor of choice

Source: "It's the Metrics That Matter," *IntelPremier IT Magazine*, Winter 2007.

organizations make better investment decisions over time. And because it is transparent, everyone learns why decisions are made and how to play their roles effectively.

The first step in the process is creating a proposal that describes benefits, costs, and risks using predefined benefit categories. Estimating the benefits that an investment will produce (if all goes well) is critical, so let's start our discussion of assessment there.

Run, grow, and transform to focus on the right benefits

The first question to be answered in assessing a proposed initiative is this: exactly how, and how much, will the investment affect and improve business performance? No single project is likely to produce every possible type of performance improvement. In fact, a common mistake made by IT organizations in justifying certain types of initiatives, such as infrastructure upgrades, is to attempt to show that such investments produce every conceivable type of benefit, from cost reduction to increased sales, even when the connection to sales and revenues is tenuous and unquantifiable. For example, how will a new Internet firewall produce value for the enterprise? Some IT organizations would attempt to make the case that the firewall will produce revenue because customers will be more likely to do business with the company via the Internet, although it's difficult to explain how and when customers consider the enterprise's firewall in making purchase decisions.

It's not necessary to tie a new firewall to revenue to show that it has plenty of value, because not everything that has value produces revenue. (Audits have value, and businesses pay plenty for them. But they don't produce revenue.) Knowing where to look for benefits helps you avoid such difficulties, and to this end it's often useful to classify initiatives by pointing to specific types of improvements in business performance.

A model developed in the early 2000s by Louis Boyle at Meta Group, and in increasing use by advisers such as Gartner and McKinsey, offers a business-oriented way to categorize investments at a high level.[2] This model classifies investments as having one of three purposes: to run, grow, or transform the business. Each classification implies different kinds of benefits.

Run-the-business investments

Run-the-business investments are about enabling essential, nondifferentiated services having the desired balance between cost and quality. Benefits are measured in reduced cost, price-to-performance ratios, and risk. Examples of run-the-business functions for most businesses include audit, payroll, and regulatory compliance. On the IT side, examples include most infrastructure investments, most IT security spending, and most IT operations spending.

Run-the-business investments do not produce revenue. They are essential to staying in business, but they don't differentiate the business in most cases. Exceptions include those cases wherein customers begin to perceive a run-the-business function as a differentiator, as appears to be happening now with "green" (environmental) initiatives and has happened recently with IT risk management and security in the financial and Internet services industries.

As noted earlier, many CIOs struggle to justify infrastructure investments, but in run-the-business terms the case is usually straightforward. First, the function is essential and typically does not need justification per se (e.g., the organization is going to be compliant with Sarbanes-Oxley in one way or another), although the level of performance required may vary (how compliant must we be?). Second, the proposed investment will deliver the best possible price for the required level of performance (e.g., it costs much less to upgrade systems over five years than to hire an army of expensive auditors annually). Price-to-performance benefits such as these are often easily and accurately calculated. The InsComp case later in this chapter provides an example.

Grow-the-business investments

Grow-the-business investments are about improvements in operations and performance related to the company's existing markets and customer segments. The value of such investments may be measured in terms of operational performance improvements, such as cycle time or improved quality, or in financial terms, such as capital expense reduction, increased revenues and margins, or reduced general and administrative (G&A) expenses. Examples include opening a new Internet or social networking channel for sales and service of existing product lines, or eliminating 10 percent from costs of conducting a key business transaction. When you're talking about improved profits or service to customers, in most cases you're talking about growing the business.

Transform-the-business investments

Transform-the-business investments are about new markets, new products, new customers—in other words, new horizons for the company, and maybe for the entire industry. Such investments are measured in prospective market share and revenues in entirely new markets. These investments typically involve big rewards and high risk. They can change the future of the company and even an industry when they succeed, or produce a large hole in the ground when they fail. Apple changed its own course and that of the music industry with iTunes; Motorola lost billions of dollars and an untold amount of alternative opportunities when the Iridium project failed.[3]

We appreciate that the word *transform* is often used in businesses to describe a lot of initiatives that would be classified as grow-the-business projects. In this classification scheme, by definition transformative initiatives involve new markets, new customer segments, and new value propositions, and not merely improved margins or profits. For example, a supply chain "transformation" that produces 40 percent increased throughput at a 30 percent reduction in costs with 20 percent improvement in quality is a grow-the-business initiative and not a transformation.

Run, grow, and transform point to specific types of benefits

These classifications aren't an end in themselves. Run, grow, and transform are not benefits; they simply point to the types of performance improvement that should be expected from an initiative and thus show you where to look for the benefits. If you say, "This is a grow-the-business initiative," it is still necessary to say exactly *how* the initiative will grow the business. Will it increase margins for a key line of business? If so, how—by reducing costs, or by increasing revenues faster than costs? Will it increase market share? If so, in which customer segments, in which markets, by how much? Will it affect soft measures of value, such as customer satisfaction, that ultimately may translate to customer retention and so to revenue? If so, how will the value be measured?

Table 6-2 summarizes some benefits that can be found for each of these classes of investment.

As an example of how these categories can help shed light on investments, consider InsComp (a pseudonym), an Asia-based subsidiary of a global financial services company with over fifty million clients and US$50 billion in revenues in 2004, of which InsComp contributed 8 percent. InsComp classifies projects in three ways: small/informal, benefit oriented, or "cost" oriented. InsComp's CIO

TABLE 6-2

Where to look for value

Type of investment	Benefit
Run the business	Price performance, risk reduction for essential nondifferentiated services that don't link to specific revenues
Grow the business	Increased revenues, reduced expenses, increased customer value in existing markets and customer segments
Transform the business	Potential revenues and market share in new markets with new customer segments and value propositions

says that "every project is treated as a business project." But different benefits approaches are employed for different types of projects.

- *Small projects* are budgeted at less than $20,000 and are funded by the business units. They are managed less formally than larger projects, meaning that identifying and tracking benefits are less rigorous. But because they are funded directly by business units, the business owners have an incentive to ensure that they realize benefits.

- *Cost projects* are initiatives that must be done as a cost of doing business, such as risk management, regulatory compliance, and some infrastructure projects. (*Cost project* is InsComp's term for run-the-business initiatives.) These projects are typically funded from the IT budget. Because they are not expected to contribute directly to profits, the projects are prioritized and measured on price-for-performance criteria: the extent to which they meet a mandated requirement within reasonable cost and risk limits. "We had a difficult project around the new national privacy regulations," says the CIO. "It was classified as a cost project. The time scales were very tight, and the regulations were very gray at the beginning. We had to get going and repeatedly adjust scope, resources, and budget against the compliance level, balancing effort required against the amount of residual risk we were prepared to live with. At the end of the day, we delivered perhaps the best solution, with balance between appropriate risk mitigation and the cost."

- *Benefit projects* are expected to improve margins and profits by delivering higher revenue or lower costs for the enterprise—grow-the-business initiatives. These investments are aggregated and prioritized based on value as measured by present value of future profits and new business contribution—two commonly used measures for investment performance in InsComp's industry. Projects are chunked into short phases to maximize traceability of expenses and benefits. "The biggest challenge is getting the business sponsor to crystallize business requirements," the CIO says. A success story was a lead management system for the sales team, which started as a US$50,000 prototype. The prototype was very well received, and InsComp invested another US$200,000 in developing a production version. After six months in production, the project produced measurable business benefits greater than fifty times the investment.

After InsComp launches a project, it is reassessed continually to ensure both timely progress against goals and the continued viability of the benefits. "I am a believer in good project management . . . the fruit of good project management is the ability to adjust when things change," says the CIO.

Run, grow, and transform are as applicable to public sector organizations as they are to the private sector. In the private sector, "grow" and "transform" refer to markets and profits; in the public sector, "grow" means extending the mission's scope (broadening the definition of the recipients of services), depth (redefining how extensively they are served), or quality. "Transform" would mean fundamentally changing the nature of the mission—for example from streamlining exploitation of public resources to conserving those resources. Figure 6-1 shows objectives, easily translated to metrics,

FIGURE 6-1

Objectives for Health and Human Services, New York City

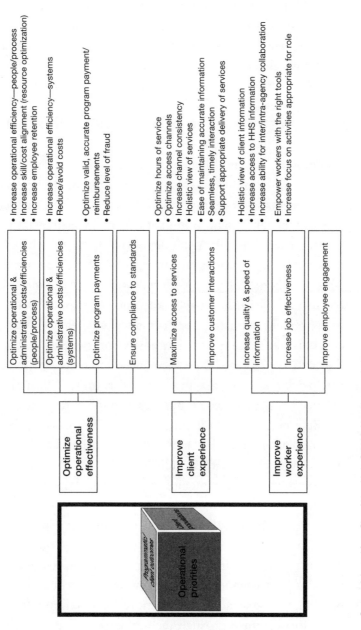

Source: Adapted from City of New York, © 2008. Used by permission.

developed by Kamal Bherwani, CIO for Health and Human Services for the City of New York, and his team in connection with the city's HHS Connect initiative. HHS Connect aims to improve health and constituent service by helping each New Yorker gain access to all health and human services for which she is eligible, through a single integrated source.

Estimate the benefits, hard and soft

The most meaningful benefits are the ones that can be measured, and the most important distinction to be made here is between *hard* benefits (whose impact can be measured in financial terms) and *soft* benefits (whose impact can be measured only in operational terms, if at all). A simple test is whether the benefit in question can be shown on a profit and loss (P&L) statement. If it can, it's a hard benefit. If not, it's soft. "Soft" does not mean worthless, but it does mean that a sponsor needs to explain exactly how an improvement in business performance will be measured. Note that concepts like "agility" are extremely soft benefits unless and until they can be tied to the performance of the enterprise in terms of the speed, risk, and cost involved in certain specific activities, such as integrating acquired companies into the enterprise.

Be especially careful about soft benefits whose quantification depends on metrics that have never been baselined. Many enterprises are currently experimenting with "social computing" channel communication strategies that are based on Web 2.0 concepts and technologies. Frequently cited benefits for these applications include enhanced collaboration, teaming, and problem solving, which arguably lead to improved productivity. But in most enterprises it is almost impossible to measure improvements in these types of performance, because few organizations (if any) have a baseline for these activities. A more likely winning argument for experimentation with such technologies is that they are the preferred channels for certain customer or employee segments—a benefit that is measurable in terms of behavior.

Be especially suspicious of the "twenty minutes per day" argument, as in "This application will reduce the time spent on XXX by twenty minutes per day." Experienced managers know that they will never see those twenty minutes hit the bottom line. By contrast, customer satisfaction is a soft benefit that can be measured in terms of net promoter scores or other survey-oriented metrics that are readily quantifiable and comparable across enterprises.[4] In some enterprises, rules of thumb exist that can be used to translate such soft benefits into financials—for example, "For every 5 percent increase in our net promoter score, history shows that we can expect a 3 percent increase in sales and a 10 percent increase in customer retention." If so, the translation can be embedded in the P&L.

Projects deliver benefits in different ways, but in an investment-oriented approach, *every* project's benefits should be identified and prioritized before it is started. In many enterprises, small projects tend to be approved with little formality and transitioned to production with little fanfare. It's easy under these conditions for everyone involved to just do the work without understanding what value the work should or does deliver.

Many IT organizations have a financial threshold for projects below which a streamlined or ad hoc prioritization process is used. If that's the case in your organization, make sure that the aggregate investment of IT's resources for all those projects is a small percentage of all the resources available for investment in IT. Overinvesting in small projects without oversight may mean that the enterprise is avoiding accountability for returns on investments in IT. In any case, if a large portion of the overall portfolio is devoted to projects whose proposed benefits are unclear at best, IT will fall into the visibility value trap: the value of IT will be much less visible, because the benefits will scarcely be visible at all.

CIOs and project sponsors are rightly wary of execution risks on large projects. It's important to remember that even when execution risks are low, as they are on most projects, realization (and recognition) of value is by no means assured.

Connect IT investment to the P&L statement

The clearest connection between IT investment and financials—and the most useful in framing discussions about where to invest—is the connection to the profit and loss (P&L) statement.

This format is clearly indicated in the hypothetical example in figure 6-2, which is taken verbatim from a public presentation by Sam Coursen in February 2008. According to Coursen—"You can't add up ROI, but you can add up P&L"—this approach is particularly useful for showing the impact of IT investment on

FIGURE 6-2

A hypothetical example of P&L impact of IT investments

Projects	Financial Metrics			P&L Business Impact (2008 – 2014)			
Project Name	IRR	Payback	NPV ($M)	Revenue Gross Margin Increase	Gross Expense Reduction	Operating Expense Reduction	Working Capital Expense
Project 1				$ 58.400	$ —	$ —	$ —
Project 2				$ —	$113.100	$ —	$ —
Project 3				$ —	$ 6.288	$ 2.695	$ —
Project 4				$ 10.146	$ —	$ —	$ —
Project 5				$ 12.950	$ —	$ —	$ —
Project 6				$ —	$ —	$ —	$ —
Project 7				$ 8.000	$ —	$ —	$ —
Project 8				$ —	$ —	$ 1.764	$ —
Project 9				$ 0.857	$ 50.889	$138.879	$ 13.972
Project 10				$ —	$ 0.630	$ 1.058	$ —
Project 11				$ —	$ —	$ —	$ —
Project 12				$ —	$ —	$ —	$ —
Project 13				$ —	$ —	$ —	$ —
Project 14				$ —	$ —	$ 0.450	$ —
Project 15							
Project 16				$ —	$ —	$ —	$ —
Project 17				$ —	$ —	$ —	$ —
Subtotal				$ 90.353	$170.907	$144.846	$ 13.972
Total P&L Benefits				$420M			

Source: Sam Coursen, Freescale Semiconductor, industry presentation, February 2008. Used by permission.

business performance across multiple business units and over time (in this hypothetical case, for the period 2008–2014). The P&L crystallizes value in terms that every business unit leader will recognize instantly. It's a terrific tool for structuring discussion around which IT investments make the most sense for the enterprise.

Each row in this statement describes the overall impact on financials of a particular project during the specified time period. Columns show internal rate of return (IRR), payback (time to recovery of the initial investment), net present value (NPV), revenue gross margin increase, gross expense reduction, operating expense reduction, and working capital expense reduction. Together, these items provide a comprehensive picture of the financial outcomes for every project for the investment period. Projects can easily be compared on any one of several bases for financial impact. This comparison is useful when, for example, there is a change in the relative importance to the business of increased revenue and reduced expenses, affecting prioritization decisions.

Obviously, this P&L statement contains a good deal of summarized information. Freescale Semiconductor uses an intermediate tool called a *business impact statement* to gather information that is then summarized for the P&L. This tool is shown in figure 6-3.

Note that this tool includes columns that allow factors contributing to the P&L for a given project—such as revenues, depreciation expenses, and reduction in the cost of capital—to be recorded year by year and line by line (in the event that the project contributes to, say, SG&A [sales, general, and administrative] expense reduction in multiple ways) for later summary in the P&L. This tool is both a guide to detailed calculation of financial benefits and a due-diligence document that allows assumptions to be tracked to the source. Because projects are assessed year by year in this format, it's particularly useful for working out the shape of returns over time, and not only the sum for a particular time period. If desired, the shape of returns compared to costs can also be charted in a graph, although we have not depicted that here.

FIGURE 6-3

Freescale Semiconductor business impact statement

Business Impact Model							
Staring Year (YYYY)	2008						
$Thousands							
Project Capital	Year 1	Year 2	Year 3	Year 4	Year 5	Comments:	
Total Project Depreciation Expense	0.0	0.0	0.0	0.0	0.0	Depreciation of project capital	
Project Non-Capital Expense	Year 1	Year 2	Year 3	Year 4	Year 5	Comments:	
Total Project Non-Capital Expense	0.0	0.0	0.0	0.0	0.0		
P&L Benefit (quantifiable benefits only)	Year 1	Year 2	Year 3	Year 4	Year 5	Comments:	Benefit Type
Gross Profit on Incremental Revenue:							
Gross profit ($) on incremental revenue	0.0	0.0	0.0	0.0	0.0		
Total Gross Profit on Incremental Revenue	0.0	0.0	0.0	0.0	0.0		
P&L Benefit (quantifiable benefits only)	Year 1	Year 2	Year 3	Year 4	Year 5	Comments:	Benefit Type
Reduced Gross Cost:							
Gross margin cost reduction	0.0	0.0	0.0	0.0	0.0		
Total Reduced Gross Cost	0.0	0.0	0.0	0.0	0.0		
P&L Benefit (quantifiable benefits only)	Year 1	Year 2	Year 3	Year 4	Year 5	Comments:	Benefit Type
Reduced Gross Cost:							
Reduced Operating Expense:							
S&GA expense reduction	0.0	0.0	0.0	0.0	0.0		
S&GA expense reduction	0.0	0.0	0.0	0.0	0.0		
Total Reduced Operating Expense	0.0	0.0	0.0	0.0	0.0		
P&L Benefit (quantifiable benefits only)	Year 1	Year 2	Year 3	Year 4	Year 5	Comments:	Benefit Type
Reduced Cost of Working Capital:							
Reduced cost of working capital	0.0	0.0	0.0	0.0	0.0		
Total Reduced Cost of Working Capital	0.0	0.0	0.0	0.0	0.0		
Total Project Benefit	0.0	0.0	0.0	0.0	0.0		

Net Cash Flow	0	0	0	0	0
Cumulative Cash Flow	0	0	0	0	0
Total Net P&L Impact	0	0	0	0	0
Cost of Capital	0				
Net Present Value	0				
Internal Rate of Return (IRR)	0				
Payback Period (Years)	N/A				

Source: Sam Coursen, Freescale Semiconductor. Used by permission.

Establish clear criteria for investment

To this point, we've discussed the tools that CIOs and initiative sponsors can use to identify and assess the value that their initiatives will provide (assuming that estimates are accurate and all goes well). But in many enterprises, assessment is not the most difficult challenge to effective prioritization of IT investments; rather, the challenge lies in the conflicting priorities and demands of business units.

IT is one of the two resources (along with money) that are often provided in most enterprises from a single resource pool. In the absence of a clear statement of priorities that supersedes the interests of particular business units, it is difficult or impossible to effectively prioritize competing interests.

In other words, expecting business unit chiefs to subordinate their priorities to other people's is reasonable only when there is a transparent investment process that allocates resources to the most important projects in the enterprise through a clearly struc-tured joint decision-making process. Otherwise, as one CIO told us, "In this kind of environment, the person who wins is often the one who shouts loudest or who makes the most convincing sales pitch, not the one who most deserves the money, and you want to avoid that."

In our research, we have seen several workable approaches for developing a transparent investment process.

- The senior team sets broad targets for investments—for example, by declaring that growth in a particular line of business, or expense reduction across all business units, is the most important priority for the time being. A variation on this approach is for senior management to carve up the investment budget in advance according to strategic priorities. Under then-CIO (now vice chairman) Joe Antonellis, State Street Corporation allocated funds

---

"About five years ago, the CEO began to bring the top BU [business unit] leaders together to foster cross-BU synergies. As the synergies emerged, it became more apparent that we were investing in duplicate systems, mostly in IT. It was a big shift from every BU owning their own systems to realizing that there were big synergies to be gained. That's when IT began showing up at the CEO's table."[5]

—Randy Spratt, CIO, McKesson

---

top-down, designating a particular percentage of the budget for each business unit or function while reserving a fund for enterprise infrastructure.

- An impartial party designated by senior management—perhaps a governance committee—ranks initiatives according to clear criteria, after which prioritized initiatives are reviewed by the senior team and reweighted as necessary. Intel has a systematic process to numerically rank projects across the enterprise, as described in greater detail later in this chapter. Projects are prioritized not only on potential financial return but also on strategic alignment and match with the enterprise's IT standards and policies.

- Initiatives are ranked by senior managers and the CIO in offline discussions and formally approved in a more public executive meeting. This approach has the benefit of reducing ongoing political infighting and streamlining the process. At Celanese, the CIO negotiates priorities one-on-one with each business unit head prior to companywide operating committee meetings.[6]

A transparent investment process need not make everyone happy. Indeed, it's a virtual certainty that to the extent that enterprise resources are limited compared with proposals for investment, someone will be disappointed. What is most important is that regardless of the investment process used, there is clarity regarding rules and decisions. This practice ensures both increased satisfaction with decisions and a reduction in attempts to game the system. A useful measure of how well the enterprise's investment process is working is to estimate the percentage of exceptions that occur through formal channels. If you and your colleagues know about most exceptions and the reasons they were granted, then your process is probably working well. But if you find out about exceptions only after the fact, then there is a hole in your process somewhere.

Sam Coursen of Freescale Semiconductor has taken this to heart. Building on his experience at NCR, he has implemented a clear process for funding and measuring each project at his new employer.

We have a very structured business model that every IT project has to follow in terms of laying out the costs of the program and the benefits. This is the Intel innovation; they have rigorously identified every category of business benefit that could exist. They map IT projects to those categories, and they track to see whether they got the benefits.

At NCR, this culture got ingrained over time. Every IT project that was over a certain amount in capital went through the business case process, where we carefully identified the benefits and costs and turned that into a P&L impact by year. For example, year 1 might have a negative P&L impact, then go positive later. You can add up all the P&L impact for a given year. You can't add up ROI, but you can add up P&L. So you can tell a business unit owner, "We're spending $20 million this year, but you'll see $100 million in P&L impact." So you get the culture thinking we don't just do projects because they're fun, but because they have a P&L impact.

You baseline the estimates. After the program is completed, you go back and estimate what you really think you're going to get now. Sometimes you audit it. Then you get better at doing the estimates over time. So you develop a culture of business value management. We had the culture at NCR; you don't do a big program without a business value management approach.

We distinguish between the hard and soft benefits. So we look at the financial benefits, but we also look at the intangibles. We don't try to turn risk assessments into dollars; that's not credible. So we keep the intangibles and the tangibles, the P&L impact, separate. It used to be that everybody esti-mated huge benefits, and nobody believed it. Now we try to be rigorous and use the Intel model to allocate benefits to categories.

I'll give you an example. We had a request to put in a Web search improvement so customers could find what they wanted more easily. Instead of simply saying, "They'll be happier, so they'll buy more," we acknowledged the diffi-culty of directly translating soft benefits into financial num-bers. We looked instead for metrics like customer satisfac-tion, number of searches, and so on—measurable stuff. If, on the other hand, you say there's a financial benefit, show me how to map it to the P&L.[7]

Intel's IT prioritization process is structured and transparent

Intel's IT prioritization process is a model of clarity and a considerable contributor to executive recognition of IT value at the company. It demands a non-trivial amount of analysis from managers, but that's neither unusual nor unexpectedly onerous for an engineering-driven company that makes a multi-billion-dollar bet every time it decides to build a chip factory.

For each proposed project, managers complete a multiple-criteria-driven checklist that examines how well the project aligns with three dimensions of merit:

- *FI,* or financial attractiveness

- *Business value,* a measure of strategic alignment

- *IT efficiency,* or the extent to which the project builds on or enhances Intel's preferred architecture

FI is about the potential financial return from the project, including new revenues and potential operating cost reductions versus the project cost. That's important but not all-important, and the other dimensions are included to lend balance to priorities. For example, a project that has a strong financial return may not be so attractive when the enterprise takes into account the project's lack of alignment with enterprise strategy, or the extent to which the project's proposed technology will impact total cost of ownership for Intel's technology base.

Because Intel IT uses the same questionnaire for all projects, it can plot every project in all three dimensions, as shown in figure 6-4. This graphic makes it very clear why some projects should be preferred over others. Intel's graphic convention is to use bubble size to represent financial attractiveness, as opposed to

FIGURE 6-4

Investment transparency at Intel

Business values

This chart shows how the BVI values of the scored projects map to the business value matrix to the right.

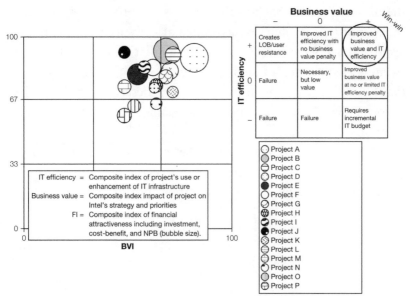

Source: Adapted from M. Curley, *Managing IT for Business Value,* Intel Press 2004. Used by permission.

positioning that rating on the X or Y axis. In this way, business value and IT efficiency are prominent; a high score in either component moves a project up and to the right.

Intel's method doesn't set priorities for projects; instead, it provides information in a transparent way for decision makers about the benefits a project offers and how it compares to the benefits offered by others. Projects outside the upper-right quadrant might still be funded. But the sponsors must clearly make a case for why a project should be chosen over others that better match the enterprise's preferred project profile.

The process also serves a key educational role. As managers start rating their projects, they come to understand how a project can be shaped to increase its value. The sponsor may choose to follow architecture rules instead of using non-standard technology. She might decide to drop a project if its value is low or unclear and focus instead on a different priority. Or she might break a project into chunks and resequence the pieces so that the project clearly hits strategic objectives.

One more step deserves mention here. Intel goes back to audit the performance of each project against its projected benefits. In other words, they harvest as systematically as they plan. This approach helps prevent managers from inflating a project's attractiveness just to get funded, and it ensures that sponsors will make every effort to achieve the benefits described in the project proposal. We discuss measuring and managing benefits in greater detail in chapter 8.

Our next chapter starts where selection and prioritization of initiatives leave off, with the elements of the virtuous cycle that are about execution and delivery.

[7]

Integrate Technology, Business Processes, and Organizational Change

MAKING GOOD IT investment decisions offers the potential for—but not the reality of—high yields. To produce actual benefits, the organization must effectively complete the elements of the virtuous cycle that are about initiative execution: business process redesign (BPR), application development (AD), and organizational change management. As with everything else we've said so far, execution is all about business performance. Building the application solution is only a small part of what's required to generate value from IT initiatives. The real value—and the real effort—lies in helping business managers identify how to change the business and then helping them play their roles in implementing those changes.

We doubt that this is news to CIOs. Indeed, there is strong evidence that CIOs recognize in particular that organizational change management is crucial to initiative success and that change management goes well beyond the CIO's scope of control. In a 2004 Meta Group survey, more than 40 percent of the 115 CIOs surveyed described culture, priorities, and politics among the three

FIGURE 7-1

CIOs say the most important barriers to change are about hearts and minds

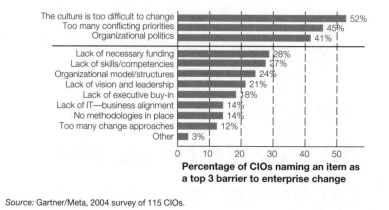

Percentage of CIOs naming an item as
a top 3 barrier to enterprise change

Source: Gartner/Meta, 2004 survey of 115 CIOs.

most important barriers to change (as shown in figure 7-1). Funding, skills, and methods were much less important.[1]

It's tempting to believe that non-IT executives, as leaders of their areas, are better able than their IT counterparts to manage change, but the evidence indicates otherwise. Recall that the non-IT executives in MIT CISR's survey cited in chapter 4 placed business process redesign (BPR) and organizational change among the IT unit's responsibilities. In the second phase of the study, 153 non-IT executives identified BPR and organization change as IT's worst-performing task (scoring 5.5 out of 10). When those executives turned the mirror on themselves, they rated themselves lowest at oversight (5.5 out of 10) and effective use of IT (5.8) but rated themselves better at strategic direction (6.7) and implementation support (6.4).[2] In short, they thought they were doing the right things, but they didn't think they were getting the right results. Clearly there is some confusion about what the "right things" are.

The difficulty is not limited to IT projects. Like IT managers, business unit managers apparently feel challenged to implement change *even in their own organizations.* In a study published in

May 2008, the Economist Intelligence Unit surveyed senior executives regarding their recent change initiatives. Four of the five most important barriers to change cited in this survey are about informal and cultural elements—winning hearts and minds and influencing behaviors of affected managers and staff—rather than implementing formal strategy and actions. No matter who is in charge or who is affected, change is hard.[3]

It's all about business performance

There is little doubt that most enterprises do application development better than they do BPR and organizational change management. There is also little doubt that most organizations have not made much progress in the recent past in dealing with organizational change. In fact, many enterprises are not yet convinced that it is really possible to systematically improve management of organizational change.[4]

Most enterprises had the same attitude toward IT project management in the 1980s and 1990s—an attitude that was always self-defeating and also turned out to be entirely wrong. IT organizations have made big strides since 1994, when the Standish Group reported that 80 percent of IT projects industrywide were partial or total failures.[5] Since then, IT organizations have changed ideas, expectations, and practices of project management. Organizations such as the Project Management Institute helped IT leaders identify and document successful practices, train practitioners, measure results, and systematically improve systems for execution.

IT leaders can and must do for organizational change management what they have done for project management. Failing to do so can destroy the credibility gained by showing value for money, and prevent the IT unit from moving farther up the path to value. This is because, when projects fail, IT more often than not pays the price, regardless of the cause. Further, this situation represents a great opportunity for IT and the CIO to solve a problem that is commonly acknowledged as serious by using systematic approaches similar to those that IT has already applied successfully to project management.

Techniques for business process redesign, application development, and organizational change have been written about extensively elsewhere (in thousands of books and articles), and we do not attempt to summarize those discussions here. Instead, we relate the main points of this book—transparency and communication—to these three elements of the virtuous cycle. We focus on establishing transparency in actions, performance, and roles so that all personnel involved in a change know what's expected and how to play their parts. It comes down to two key elements:

1. Systematically identify BPR and organizational change requirements up front in every initiative.

2. Build transparency and learning into the entire execution process.

Systematically examine all dimensions of change from the start

Many companies have learned to examine the potential risks and requirements of application development, but fewer have fully integrated organizational change and BPR into these assessments. Intel has made significant progress in this regard in its IT innovation efforts. As part of the IT innovation team's innovation delivery process, managers examine six dimensions of change:

1. The vision of the problem or opportunity

2. The solution and how it is enabled via IT

3. The business case for change

4. Internal business process change

5. Internal organizational change

6. Customer adoption, which often requires customer or societal changes

Each "vector" must be carefully managed to ensure the innovation delivers the promised benefit.

The starting point is gaining a clear *vision* of how a particular opportunity can be exploited or how a particular problem can be solved with support from IT. The *business case*—showing whether and how the innovation will pay returns beyond the investment—is often more difficult to identify than the potential IT solution.[6]

The other three dimensions are about change in business processes, organization, and customer behaviors. These soft issues are often the most difficult of all. Changing a business process requires much more than formally rerouting tasks or eliminating process steps. It requires changes in behaviors, roles, and organizational structures and incentives that do not show up on a process flowchart. These organizational changes, because they involve attention to people and not just technology, require the greatest managerial skill to address. And failing to address them can be far more damaging than a mistake in process design.

Finally, many initiatives may succeed only if they are adopted externally—by customers, suppliers, regulators, partners, or other stakeholders. If reshaping or external informing is the means to create new value (see chapter 5), then the value will not be achieved unless external customers or partners adopt the change. If the initiative helps customers conduct their existing processes more effectively or more easily with little effort or change, it is likely to be adopted quickly. But when external stakeholders must invest in new technology, skills, capabilities, or processes—as when Wal-Mart required its supply chain partners to adopt radio frequency identification (RFID) technology—then initiative managers must find the means to facilitate those changes.

Intel's six dimensions expose the risks and opportunities—as opposed to the technology alone—that are present in process, organization, and customer change. They help managers know, in advance, what to expect and provide signposts to help manage delivery of benefits from the innovation.

Systematizing business process redesign

CIOs know how important BPR is. The work of Hammer and Champy, among others, popularized the concept in the 1980s and 1990s.[7] Consulting practices were formed to facilitate BPR, and IT has always played a major part.

Process is the dominant paradigm for all of IT, and the CIO is often acknowledged by the executive team as the first or second most knowledgeable person in the enterprise where business processes are concerned. CIOs certainly know that there's more risk than value in IT-supported initiatives to automate processes that haven't been carefully thought through beforehand.

Surprisingly, though, despite more than two decades of industry practice relatively few enterprises do BPR well. The CIO who can improve BPR on all projects, therefore, has an opportunity to deliver more value than competitors who don't—and improving BPR starts with adopting a systematic approach to up-front problem analysis. We share two ways that CIOs have helped their enterprises systematically improve BPR.

One approach is to create a small team to do rapid business process analysis before IT work begins. DirectEnergy's CIO Kumud Kalia formed a small team of MBAs from top business schools to serve as business process analysts. He sends the analysts to work with business unit executives to analyze chronic business problems. The analysts examine a whole business process, end to end, to diagnose root causes of long-standing problems and then propose solutions. The team usually identifies multiple options that accomplish what the business wants and more, with the added benefits of smoother process flow, lower operational costs, and improved functionality. This may or may not require follow-on IT investment—Kalia believes that avoiding a major IT expense by reengineering business processes is legitimate value-add, allowing him to focus IT attention on where it will have the most impact. The whole exercise takes less than three months—a small investment compared to the savings and opportunities they identify.

Other CIOs have added specific BPR steps to their system development life cycles. CIO Al-Noor Ramji and his team at British Telecom (BT) developed the hothouse concept to ensure joint IT and business unit involvement in process redesign from the start of major projects. Hothouses bring together a variety of experts, from IT and non-IT roles, into a fast-paced, full-time workshop environment. The goal is to find the best design for a new process. "For three days we build three prototypes with six to eight competing teams," Ramji says. "It's not a question of IT guys versus businesspeople; every professional skill set has to turn up and do it. And that's been a huge revolution, because working your own pieces and doing your own thing accurately doesn't help when the customer's at stake. And no department is sufficient to give the customer an end-to-end service. All of us are necessary."[8]

Whether you use a team of analysts to think through the impact and implications of process change, the BPR effort pays off in more than just better designs. Each successful BPR exercise shows business executives the importance and power of thinking about their side of things—the business process—in addition to the system itself. Further, each iteration increases the IT unit's knowledge of the business and gives IT leaders additional credibility as contributors to business and strategy discussions.

In many cases this practice gains IT increased responsibility for business processes as well as technology. For example, Solectron CIO Bud Mathaisel also served as the enterprise's chief process officer, with responsibility for IT *and* business process effectiveness. He visited customers regularly and worked with executives throughout the business to sponsor initiatives that made the company easier to do business with. Still other IT leaders, having implemented new processes, are asked to take over operations for those processes in addition to their IT responsibilities. We examine these extended roles and others in chapter 9.

Systematizing organizational change

Systematic management of organizational change is not necessarily more difficult than application development and BPR, but it is more often ignored. Gartner estimates that fewer than 15 percent of enterprises have established roles and organizational structures explicitly charged with managing and facilitating organizational change, compared with the 40 percent (as high as 90 percent in some regions, such as Australia) of enterprises that have established a project management office.[9]

This behavior is shortsighted in the extreme, because of all the risks associated with change, resistance from the people affected by the change is the most predictable. The first reaction of almost any person confronted with almost any change is to resist it. Resistance is normal and predictable even when change is apparently desirable—such as a promotion or the birth of a child—and especially when the change seems to be imposed from outside. Further, resistance generally takes a predictable form over time.[10]

In short, managers must expect and manage the cycle of resistance to change, because resistance will surely occur whether or not it is anticipated and managed.

There are systematic ways to examine the potential for resistance and to include those considerations in project plans. For more than ten years, MIT Sloan School of Management faculty have been teaching their students a model of organizational change. The model examines change requirements using three different lenses: formal, political, and cultural (see figure 7-2).[11]

Formal design (also called strategic design) includes the elements of an organization that are most readily written or drawn on charts. It includes structure and roles, business processes, management systems, incentives, formal strategies, and policies. New IT applications, business process changes, and organizational structures all affect formal design. Changes to formal design are often simplest to plan, because they can be rationally engineered based on the requirements of an initiative. But such changes often

FIGURE 7-2

Three perspectives on organizations and change

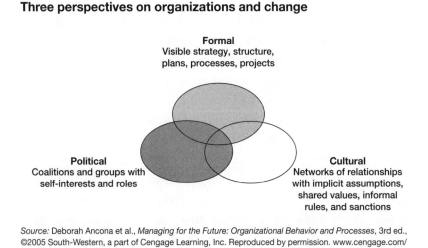

Formal
Visible strategy, structure,
plans, processes, projects

Political
Coalitions and groups with
self-interests and roles

Cultural
Networks of relationships
with implicit assumptions,
shared values, informal
rules, and sanctions

Source: Deborah Ancona et al., *Managing for the Future: Organizational Behavior and Processes*, 3rd ed.,
©2005 South-Western, a part of Cengage Learning, Inc. Reproduced by permission. www.cengage.com/
permissions.

have effects on the other two perspectives that result in increased resistance from the people affected by the change.

The *political* lens examines the sources and uses of power in the organization: who has it, where it comes from, how it is used. Those who believe that their power will be eroded as a result of the change typically resist, often indirectly. But just as important is the unintentional resistance that happens from goal conflict, when the goals of the initiative run counter to the (stated or unstated) goals of the organization units and their members. CIOs and other leaders should recognize, up front, who is likely to gain and lose power, and where conflicting goals may exist, so they can take steps to address resulting resistance as soon as possible.

Culture is the system of shared values and beliefs held by members of the organization. The culture of an organization is often so deeply ingrained that it is unconscious and almost invisible to insiders. But it weaves through everything the organization does. It affects every assumption people make about what is possible or permissible, from the ways dissenters are handled to the products and services that can be offered to customers. Although a strong culture can be highly effective (consider the cultures of Southwest Airlines or USAA or Apple), it can also dangerously undermine change when change calls for values and behaviors that run counter to those of the prevailing culture. For example, Polaroid was unable to adapt to digital photography, even though the company had the technology to do it, largely because its culture rejected any product that did not come with a renewable component (such as film) that they could continue to sell to customers long after the sale of the camera itself. And many professional service businesses had trouble adapting to service or billing models, such as fixed price or offshore. Assessing the organizational change requirements of a new initiative, then, is a systematic process of examining how the new world at the end of the project will differ from the existing world according to each lens, and then taking steps to address the differences. This exercise should be integrated with all other project planning, because the formal design of processes and technology may well present painful changes in the political and cultural lenses.

Some cultural issues can be managed through effective communication; indeed, in interviews in 2005, managers at Cisco, a company that has built its change capabilities in part through experience in numerous acquisitions, told us that they spend 50 to 80 percent of their time in major change initiatives communicating with the sponsors and targets of change.[12] Political issues can be managed by adjusting formal design to realign structure or incentives. But sometimes it takes more direct and dramatic action, such as when the new senior team at Tektronix addressed political resistance to a global restructuring of processes and supporting systems by restructuring to eliminate the company's powerful country managers.[13] Successful executives use techniques such as those described here to understand the potential risks of organizational change early and to work with other authorities to address them effectively.

Strong leadership to address resistance to change is essential. Strong leaders establish vision and communication to unite the organization around a common goal. They also know when to take strong action to force change. It's remarkable how often managers of successful initiatives describe a defining moment when resistance was broken and the future of the project ensured. Nestlé's worldwide sales process restructuring, called Project Globe, came at a time when the firm was doing well financially, but investment analysts demanded more. Passive resistance by powerful sales executives had turned to open hostility to the initiative when project manager Chris Johnson took the offensive in a global sales meeting. Johnson explained that if the project failed, he might lose his job, but responsibility would then fall to one of the sales executives to make it succeed. The initiative was important to the CEO and it was going to happen, no matter who ran it. This meeting, combined with the CEO's consistent support for Johnson and the project, went a long way to quell political resistance from local executives who feared they would lose power to headquarters.

Because BPR and organizational change management are essential to nearly every initiative, IT project management offices are often the first organizations in an enterprise to develop change management expertise. CIOs can take advantage of IT's reputation for project management, which is often acknowledged throughout the enterprise, to champion management of organizational change, beginning by incorporating funds and activities for change management into every major project. In other words, this is one aspect of the virtuous cycle in which IT can lead, even if IT doesn't control all the resources involved. IT will benefit as much or more than any other group as a result.

Former Selectron CIO Bud Mathaisel charged his project management office not only with monitoring project status but also with ensuring that business unit personnel assigned to the project played their parts by attending meetings, reviewing work in progress, and ensuring that the business unit was prepared to implement new processes. This program has visibly improved success rates for projects. "Our PMO is such a valuable entity that it's now being emulated by other groups in our company," Mathaisel says. "We have lost people to other groups . . . they've hired them away (at our encouragement) to go and take program management mind-sets into those other organizations."[14]

Build transparency and learning
into project execution

Understanding and managing requirements for process and organizational change are necessary practices but not sufficient for success. Without efficient and effective project execution, value will be reduced or lost. As in the preceding section, we focus here not on specific details of project management but on two ways to ensure that project execution is transparent in methods, roles, and performance for everyone participating.

The first is to make the project's methods and roles as clear as possible to all players. This is the role of a well-structured software development life cycle (SDLC) methodology, which specifies, for an initiative of a given type, what must be done, by whom, in what order, and with what expected outcomes and deliverables. Given the improvements in project success rates over the past decade (as described earlier in this chapter), it is clear that most CIOs now understand the importance of a good SDLC. Those who don't should know that it is a critical component of ensuring that the risks associated with application development—not only of availability and access but also of accuracy and agility—are well managed.[15] CIOs should also know that a study based on data from more than fifteen thousand projects published by Gartner in 1997 found that projects using a moderately rigorous methodology were on average 35 percent more productive than projects using none.[16]

SDLC methodologies vary in detail and rigor. The most important rule is to make them proportional to the complexity of the project and the skills of the team. To land a plane, an airline pilot needs only a checklist taped to the instrument panel in the cockpit, because the pilot is already well trained and experienced and needs only a reminder to execute each step of the landing in order. Similarly, a well-trained project manager executing a familiar type of project with a skilled team needs little more than a checklist to ensure success. But when complexity or project requirements take a project beyond the familiar, rigor should increase, or else your risks will multiply.

The second approach to improving transparency for application development is in-process oversight, which means regularly bringing together executives from IT and the rest of the business to make key decisions. As the project reaches each gate in a series, the project is reviewed with sponsors, the project team, and the project management office for progress against goals and key risks. Each gate calls for a go–no go decision for the next stage of activity and funding.[17] This process helps ensure that projects don't begin or continue when large, unaddressed risks are present.

But a gated SDLC can also be a source of frustration for business executives. The issues managed at each gate, and the process to manage them, can be daunting to someone who doesn't have a strong technical background. Busy executives who don't understand the rationale or assumptions for key decision points can be excused for feeling unhappy. These normally highly competent individuals are asked to make decisions for which they lack expertise or are asked to slow their units' plans to ensure that (from their point of view) IT's demands are satisfied. Neither is a useful way to build collegiality between IT and the rest of the business. In other words, a gated SDLC process can throw IT into the IT-is-an-obstruction value trap.

Raytheon Global CIO Rebecca Rhoads found a way to avoid being perceived as an obstruction. Rather than make business executives learn a separate SDLC language for IT, she and her staff put all IT decisions into the same process (Integrated Product Development System, or IPDS) that Raytheon uses for all its major capital programs (see figure 7-3). IPDS, Raytheon's standard engineering project milestone methodology, is in use at any given time on about eight thousand engineering projects at the company. Large projects go through all gates, whereas smaller projects go through a streamlined process consisting of fewer gates. Either way, the gates match the gates already in use by the rest of the business.

Putting IT projects into IPDS shows that they are as important as any other engineering project and that they use the same

FIGURE 7-3

Raytheon–IT governance links to the companywide Integrated Product Development System (IPDS)

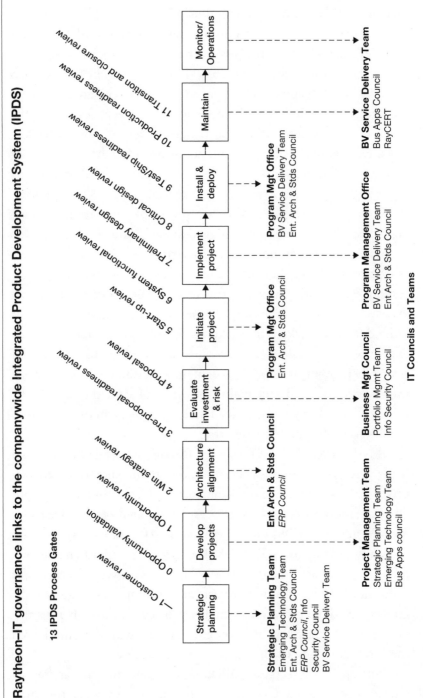

13 IPDS Process Gates

-1 Customer review
0 Opportunity validation
1 Opportunity review
2 Win strategy review
3 Pre-proposal readiness review
4 Proposal review
5 Start-up review
6 System functional review
7 Preliminary design review
8 Critical design review
9 Test/Ship readiness review
10 Production readiness review
11 Transition and closure review

Strategic planning → **Develop projects** → **Architecture alignment** → **Evaluate investment & risk** → **Initiate project** → **Implement project** → **Install & deploy** → **Maintain** → **Monitor/Operations**

Strategic Planning Team
Emerging Technology Team
Ent. Arch & Stds Council
ERP Council, Info
Security Council
BV Service Delivery Team

Ent Arch & Stds Council
ERP Council

Business Mgt Council
Portfolio Mgmt Team
Info Security Council

Program Mgt Office
Ent. Arch & Stds Council

Program Mgt Office
BV Service Delivery Team
Ent. Arch & Stds Council

Project Management Team
Strategic Planning Team
Emerging Technology Team
Bus Apps council

Program Management Office
BV Service Delivery Team
Ent Arch & Stds Council

BV Service Delivery Team
Bus Apps Council
RayCERT

IT Councils and Teams

Source: Raytheon Corporation. Used with permission.

techniques and rigor. Rhoads says that this integration has paid tremendous benefits in process and participation. "[We use the] same structure, same language, same players. And when you get to that point, then they feel like they're involved, and they know how to be involved . . . If you invite them to the meeting and then you talk IT language, they're not sure how to contribute, which is going to frustrate them. But if you bring them to a gate review, like any project gate review, that's structured in a way the person knows . . . what we're supposed to do with that particular gate and what role they play, then . . . you've got them as a teammate."[18]

Integrating IT into IPDS does more than improve communication; it creates links to the company culture. Managing IT projects according to the same process that executives already know helps all stakeholders play their roles more easily. Everyone knows what a gate 5 review is and what it means to pass one. And everyone understands that it's all right to fail a gate, because that happens all the time in many parts of the business. A gate is not an audit review that spells potential doom for a project and its manager. Rather, it is a checkpoint to help everyone understand that a project has addressed certain key requirements. Failure means going back and getting it right so that progress can continue, just as for all the other projects in the company.

Reviews should be frequent to ensure learning and reduce risk. If an organization learns that a project is failing only when it misses its final deadline, the company has wasted time, money, and opportunities. What's worse, had managers understood sooner that the project was in trouble, they might have been able to take action to fix it before it failed.

BT CIO Al-Noor Ramji has implemented a straightforward, effective approach to improve the speed of learning about project performance. "We . . . make sure every one of them [projects] delivers every ninety days, and if it doesn't deliver, the post-implementation review process will cut it off." Managers are encouraged to chunk their projects into smaller parts that can deliver meaningful functionality in ninety days. Reviews examine the roles everyone played in the performance of the project. And managers' annual incentive bonuses are based on participation in quarterly reviews, and not only the success of their projects. The ninety-day review process has been effective in improving the company's ability to deliver on investments and manage resources across programs.

With needs assessment, transparent investment, and the integration of AD, BPR, and organizational change management complete, the only element of the virtuous cycle remaining is measurement of the value delivered—what we call the harvest. That's the subject of the next chapter, which concludes our discussion of how CIOs can successfully position IT as an investment in business performance.

$$\left[\; 8 \;\right]$$

Measure the Value Delivered

WE'VE SAID IT BEFORE: players know the score. The last part of the virtuous cycle is about keeping score, and in this case you keep score by tallying the actual value delivered by an investment in IT. Did the business case (as described in the project proposal) estimate a reduction in head count, an increase in sales of a particular product, or a reduction in the cost of a manufacturing process? This is the part of the virtuous cycle in which the enterprise determines whether those benefits were delivered. Measuring the benefits ensures that IT, along with initiative sponsors, gets credit for improving business performance.

In addition to ensuring that the value proposed by the business case is realized, measuring the value ensures that the enterprise will learn to estimate the benefits of initiatives more accurately. This accuracy, in turn, improves the planning and investment process and drives up yields from investments in IT. When sponsors know that the actual benefits will be counted, they're less likely to inflate the benefits to promote a project. When they do, decision makers will know it and can take it into account when the next proposal arrives.

Enterprises have good reasons to measure benefits, even if most don't measure now

Those are the good reasons for measuring benefits, and they are very good indeed. But apparently they are not good enough for many enterprises. Measuring the value delivered by initiatives that involve IT is a practice that most businesses have not adopted. The not-for-profit JUAS (Japan Users Association of Information Systems) estimated in a 963-participant survey in 2004 that only 13 percent of Japanese companies with revenues greater than $1 billion consistently ran post-implementation benefits realization analyses. The figure dropped to 7 percent for all sizes of companies in the sample.[1]

We are not surprised by those numbers. First, it is a matter of habit. Even when enterprises are accustomed to keeping score on investments in plant and equipment or real estate, few are used to doing so where IT is concerned. The effort involved is not especially onerous, but it may seem like a lot to an enterprise that has never expended effort on the matter.

Further, not all managers actually *want* to measure the results of their investments in IT. In fast-growing companies in particular, managers are focused on seizing opportunities, not on keeping score. They figure that the score will take care of itself if they pursue as many opportunities as possible, and IT's resources in many cases seem less real and less limited than their own. This is especially so when demand management mechanisms like governance are immature. To these managers, measuring benefits seems like an invitation to refuse funding for future projects that otherwise are sure to be approved.[2]

Many managers simply feel that major IT investments are extremely risky, and they don't want to be held accountable for delivering the benefits when they feel they can't control the outcomes. And it is cynical, but probably true, to say that if the benefits do not appear, IT will most often be held accountable. A 2004 survey by Gartner and Forbes.com found that 94 percent of

CEOs held IT responsible for project failures.[3] In general, the closer an executive was to the CEO on the organization chart, the likelier it was that the executive blamed IT when failure occurred. So why should anyone else volunteer to take on the risk?

CIOs can't afford not to measure the benefits of investment in IT

These are serious arguments, and CIOs need to move beyond them. Failing to measure benefits is a variation on the "IT only delivers technology" value trap that separates IT from any yields produced by investment. Companies often have structured investment processes (and sometimes measurement processes) for their capital investments. Why should investments involving IT be any different? And companies can address the risks of delivery by improving application development, BPR, and organizational change management, as described in chapter 7.

The problem is that, as with other parts of the virtuous cycle, IT can't simply go forward on its own. Measuring benefits requires participation of everyone involved in an initiative, inside and outside IT. This is true in particular because the value of any investment in IT that is not purely infrastructural is not expressed in the IT budget. The value is expressed in business performance.

For example, the CIO of a large U.S. health care organization manages an IT budget that represents about 4 percent of enterprise revenue. This ratio—about twice the typical IT budget for the half-dozen companies that the company's management considers peers—is large enough to get the attention of executives and industry analysts. When the IT budget is the only thing under consideration, IT looks expensive at this company.

However, G&A expenses for the company run about 10 percent of revenues, compared with a range of 18 percent to 30 percent in the peer group. To put it another way, the extra 2 percent of revenue spent on IT has reduced the percentage of revenue for G&A expenses by 8 to 20 percent, increasing margins compared with

"We might have a quality measurement that says we'll improve picking accuracy. The IT investment is considered in light of that goal. There might be other factors needed to achieve the goal as well, such as process changes or incentive plan changes. We measure the quality of the outcome of our investments. We go back repeatedly, up to two years after implementation, to make sure that we get the value."[4]

—John Hammergren, CEO, McKesson

peers. Much of this reduction in business cost is the result of recent investment in electronic records management, which has driven up the IT budget while significantly reducing the amount of time, effort, and quality control that is needed to manage the huge volume of records that any health care business handles daily.[5]

That is exactly what an investment is supposed to do: apply a relatively small amount of resources to create a larger positive outcome. When the outcomes are outside the IT budget—and we trust we have made it clear by now that when things are going in the right direction, that is exactly where the outcomes are located—then the only way to measure the value of the investment in IT is by looking at business performance.

Creating the conditions for a successful harvest

To use an agricultural metaphor, the first stage of the virtuous cycle—needs identification and investment planning—is like preparing the ground. Business process redesign, application development, and organizational change management are like planting the seeds and tending the fields. The last step is to manage the harvest—to ensure that the effort and resources that have gone into planning and execution bear fruit and produce value.

The participation of everyone involved in an initiative is necessary for a successful harvest, and for its own good IT needs to ensure that everyone involved commits to do what is necessary to achieve and measure the benefits. As a practical matter, the single leverage point at which IT organizations can most compellingly present the requirement for post-implementation measurement of benefits is the point at which a project is approved and just before it is provisioned. At that point, the momentum leading to initiation of the project is powerful. Sponsors are prepared to lead, resources are under active consideration, and the benefits seem tangible. CIOs can use that momentum to ask project participants to affirm their commitment to delivering and measuring value by participating in post-project reviews of benefit harvest. Few sponsors will refuse in those circumstances, when the project—for which so much time and political capital have been expended—seems imminent and the benefits reviews seem far off. This is especially so because refusal will appear to cast doubt on the credibility of the benefit estimates.

A successful value harvest requires three things in particular.

- *Clear expectations for benefits:* If the opportunity assessment and investment decision process are working reasonably well, there should be little doubt at this point about exactly what an initiative is supposed to deliver and which measures of performance, operational or financial, will apply. If that's not so, then the assessment and investment processes are broken, and the CIO should use her influence to help fix them.

- *Baseline measurements of the financial or operational performance areas that are the targets of the initiative:* Again, these should have been established during opportunity identification and assessment. If not, IT can do what Intel's and other IT leaders do: work with finance and other areas of the company to identify the right numbers and baseline them.

- *A structured post-implementation review process:* This review is focused on improvements in business performance, and the duration and rigor of this process are proportional to the project's size and scope. This is the harvest machinery that most organizations don't have, and it isn't accounted for by earlier phases of the virtuous cycle. This process, and related best practices in benefit realization, is the focus of the rest of this chapter.

Creating the harvest steering group

Ensuring that value is delivered is a process, and a process must be managed. After IT solutions are delivered and business change is complete, the project steering group is replaced by the *harvest steering group*.

Two of the most important functions of any steering group are to manage risk and make decisions. Because the decisions and risks involved in the harvest differ from those involved in the execution phase, membership of the steering group may also change between the two phases. Typical members of a harvest steering group include the business sponsor, key internal users, the CFO or a designated CFO representative, and IT development and operations staff. IT personnel on the steering group often shift from senior development staff during execution to senior operations staff during the harvest. The CFO usually takes a stronger role in the harvest steering group than in development and often is the chair. Figure 8-1 shows typical harvest steering group roles, responsibilities, and activities.

The harvest steering group for a project should stay alive until the business changes delivered during execution become part of business as usual. The group meets periodically to look for deviations from the benefit plan, to advise the business and IT operations staff on any needed remedial actions, and to escalate serious

FIGURE 8-1

Evolve the project governance team into a harvest steering group

Typical harvest steering group activities and responsibilities

- Stays alive until benefits realization becomes part of business as usual
- Conducts periodic reviews of benefits realized versus planned — transition frequency from monthly to quarterly to annually
- Advises business process owner/users where benefits are going off track or business changes threaten benefits
- Reports to business executives where significant deviation occurs
- Commissions a benefits audit during the harvest phase using nonproject resources

Typical steering group roles

Business sponsor	Overall accountability for realization of benefits
CFO	Detailed auditing of benefits realization, also often enforcer and link to board
Key customers	Feedback whether needs are being met and how to improve
CIO and IS managers	Diagnose IS issues related to harvest, and identify fixes, capture learning regarding IT practices

issues to the executive committee. Exact intervals between meetings depend on the size and complexity of the project and associated business changes, with bigger projects typically involving longer intervals. This group should also commission a benefit audit, as described later in this chapter.

Measurement includes four major components

The overall process of managing the measurement and benefit harvest phase is shown in figure 8-2. Steps include the following:

1. Start-up

2. Periodic harvest reviews

3. Harvest audit

4. Completion of harvest

Let's discuss these in order.

FIGURE 8-2

Manage the entire harvest phase

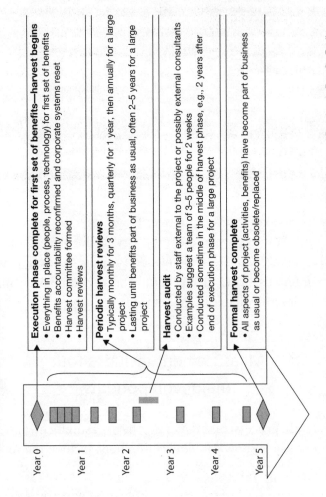

Execution phase complete for first set of benefits—harvest begins
- Everything in place (people, process, technology) for first set of benefits
- Benefits accountability reconfirmed and corporate systems reset
- Harvest committee formed
- Harvest reviews

Periodic harvest reviews
- Typically monthly for 3 months, quarterly for 1 year, then annually for a large project
- Lasting until benefits part of business as usual, often 2–5 years for a large project

Harvest audit
- Conducted by staff external to the project or possibly external consultants
- Examples suggest a team of 3–5 people for 2 weeks
- Conducted sometime in the middle of harvest phase, e.g., 2 years after end of execution phase for a large project

Formal harvest complete
- All aspects of project (activities, benefits) have become part of business as usual or become obsolete/replaced

Year 0
Year 1
Year 2
Year 3
Year 4
Year 5

Source: Dave Aron, Chuck Tucker, and Richard Hunter, "Show Me the Money: Advanced Practices in Benefits Realization," Gartner Executive Programs Signature Report, December 2005.

Start-up

Most enterprises implement some kind of review when the implementation phase of a project is complete. Such reviews are desirable; MIT CISR surveys have shown that enterprises that do post-implementation reviews (PIRs) better than others get higher business value from IT. Many such reviews are run by the IT team, and so the focus tends to be on IT's performance as opposed to the readiness of the business to reap value. In a traditional PIR, questions typically include these:

- Did IT deliver the promised functionality in the right time period?

- Were costs managed effectively?

- Where didn't this happen, and why not?

- Are there lessons to be learned for next time?

Although this kind of review is necessary and desirable, it's not sufficient. Post-implementation reviews must go beyond IT's performance on the project up to the point of system delivery. Attendees should include all key stakeholder groups, including business sponsor, users, IT delivery team, program and change management team, and IT operations.

Further, even though lessons learned from the delivery effort are important, the review must go further to ask whether the business is in a position to reap the expected benefits, and whether benefit goals need to be reset because it is now clear that initial goals were unrealistically high or low. This discussion should cover whether any remedial action can or should be taken to recover the benefit position and whether any new benefit opportunities have arisen that should be fed into the portfolio process.

This review is a good time to reaffirm ownership and accountability of benefits and to ensure that management goals, such as budgets and head counts, are appropriately reset (as described in detail a bit later). Finally, a schedule for continuing benefit reviews should be set at the post-implementation review. In other words, the function of this meeting is to level-set and prepare everyone for continuing assessment of the value delivered by the initiative.

Table 8-1 compares a traditional IT-run post-implementation review with a benefit-focused post-implementation review.

Reset management processes to set the stage for benefits

However accurate benefit measures are, if they simply exist in a business case, they probably won't affect business users' behaviors. Benefits tend to leak away. Partial head-count reductions (for example, half a person) often disappear, and substantial head-count reductions may end up with staff moving to other areas rather than actually being cut. Failure to meet revenue uplifts is often blamed on changes in external factors, such as competitors' campaigns, during project execution.

If, however, benefits are baked in to the mainstream management processes that drive the business (see figure 8-3), where named individuals are responsible for delivering on those systems, there is much more clarity and motivation in pursuing those benefits.

Budgets, head counts, scorecards, and incentives are the most common management processes that should integrate benefits. One challenge is that these process targets typically are set at fixed times, often semiannually or annually. Baking benefits in might require resetting these targets out of cycle.

This is a benefit of having the CFO staff involved. They can adjust budget and adjudicate estimates so that the CIO doesn't need to.

Periodic harvest reviews

Periodic reviews are held to measure progress toward achievement of benefits and to determine whether action is needed, and by whom, to correct risks or maximize opportunities. Here, as in the initial review, the benefit estimates contained in the approved proposal are the most important guide to what should be measured.

TABLE 8-1

Ensure that a post-implementation review is focused on benefits

Element	Traditional IS wrap-up meeting characteristics	Benefits-focused post-implementation review additional characteristics
Involvement	Variable, depending on availability	All key stakeholders, including internal customers, business sponsor, CIO, development team, program and change management team, IS operations, any external partner/ customers
Scope	IS delivery	Enterprise ability to harvest benefits
Discussion points	• Was functionality delivered as requested? Are internal customers satisfied that we have delivered? • Was system delivered on time and to budget? • Which technologies/ approaches worked well/ badly?	• How has the reality of the execution phase impacted benefits? Have external factors (e.g., unexpected competitor actions) changed the benefit equation? Do benefit estimates need to be changed? • Is the business now in the position to harvest the benefits? If not, are there remedial actions to be taken? • Are there unexpected business opportunities that have arisen during the execution phase? • What best practices and pitfalls can be captured and communicated to improve future initiatives?
Outputs	• Input into IS scorecards/ reports • Input into IS knowledge base re development techniques	• Accountability and commitment to (modified) benefits, with agreement to embed into corporate systems • Proposals for remedial/ opportunistic projects • Agreed-to harvest steering committee, review, and audit schedule

Source: Dave Aron, Chuck Tucker, and Richard Hunter, "Show Me the Money: Advanced Practices in Benefits Realization," Gartner Executive Programs Signature Report, December 2005.

FIGURE 8-3

Bake benefits into corporate systems and processes

- Benefits such as cost reduction, revenue increases, and staff reduction are often subject to "leakage."
- *Resetting* major corporate systems, processes, and budgets enforces accountability and focuses the minds of all stakeholders.

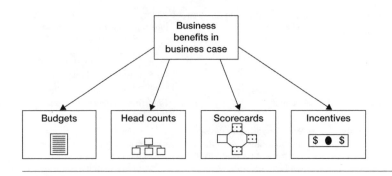

Reviewers should also be alert to signs of additional hard or soft benefits or costs not envisioned in the proposal. (The law of unintended consequences cuts both ways.) For example, at British Petroleum, implementation of automatic level readings for customers' liquefied natural gas (LNG) tanks allowed the company to serve those customers on an as-needed basis, reducing costs for both parties. An unanticipated soft benefit was that customers stopped worrying about whether they were about to run out of LNG. In effect, BP outsourced the customers' anxiety to itself, and that measurably increased customer satisfaction with BP's services.[6]

Independent harvest audit

Over time, the circumstances that were part of estimates may change drastically, and it may be impossible to realize benefits calculated carefully in good faith. Whatever the reason, it's important to know why estimates were or were not valid so you can improve future estimates and the use of those estimates in investment decisions.

Although the aim of harvest reviews is to maximize benefit from the project, a harvest audit is conducted primarily to learn what worked and what didn't work in generating value for the enterprise. The key activities of the audit group are measuring the benefits, comparing them to the plan, and researching the root causes of variances. This work results in a set of best practices and issues to avoid or address early.

Characteristics of a harvest audit include the following:

- *Timing:* Ideally, the harvest audit should be conducted well into the harvest phase so that the realities of harvest are stable and clearly visible. A good time is one year after business and IT changes have been deployed.

- *Effort:* The size of the team and the duration of the audit depend on the size and complexity of the project. For example, for a $3 million to $5 million ERP project in a $1 billion enterprise that took two years to implement, a typical audit would comprise a team of three to five people conducting a ten-day to two-week audit.

- *Team:* The team should comprise people who have extensive knowledge of the business functions, financial functions, and IT areas that are important to the project. The audit team should also be independent of the project team that developed the systems and process changes. Often a good choice is a team from another geographic or business unit that is familiar with the context but relatively independent.

Completion of harvest

Recent research found that, on average, the returns to IT-supported initiatives (in terms of productivity and output growth) were measurable after one year and then accelerated over time. They were two to five times as large after seven years.[7] Reasons for the long ramp-up include the many years it takes for companies to implement complementary organizational and process changes that can make the most of the technology investment. Diminishing returns will occur later, as the incremental value of continuous improvement peaks. Then, companies may need more radical change to get to the next performance plateau.

This means that for larger initiatives especially, expectations of benefits should take the lag into account. Reviews should not be expected to show substantial benefits for as much as one year for such initiatives. Once benefits are apparent, measurement might continue for as long as five years, or until the enterprise is satisfied that the gains from the initiative are now part of business as usual.

Putting the virtuous cycle together

You don't need to be a large, technology-focused enterprise to improve the virtuous cycle, nor is perfection necessary. Consider the process used by the North American subsidiary of $5.86 billion (as of YE 2008) global paper manufacturer Sappi Limited. Sappi NA improved discipline through a major initiative aimed at standardizing processes, supported by ERP technology, in 2005.[8]

North America VP of procurement and CIO Bob Wittstein worked on all phases of the virtuous cycle when implementing the ERP. As developed in 2005 and continuously refined since, benefit identification is tailored depending on each project's strategic goal. For infrastructure projects, IT sets budget aside and does a less extensive cost benefit analysis; for capital purchases, there is a more formal process. For projects directly related to customer service or innovation, Wittstein notes, there is no point in doing painstaking benefit analyses; the decision has already been made. However, for operational excellence initiatives, which normally mean cost reduction, it makes sense to do thorough benefit planning and follow-up. Finally, for disaster-recovery planning projects, Wittstein uses a justification based on the business impacts of systems outages over time.

Previously, Sappi executives had an unfavorable perception of benefit realization. "I used to expect IT projects to take twice as long and cost twice as much," says Mark Gardner, president and CEO. "That was because there was less rigor; IT sat outside the capital requirements process."

Execution is also improved through disciplined project management. And BPR is part of every project. Sappi created a business process engineering group made up of user experts for each functional area (who report directly to the functional area VPs) plus their IT counterparts. Wittstein explains:

> This group is now called the Cross Functional Team [CFT]. Project sponsors fill out a form describing the project's goals, benefits, and ROI. That form goes to the CFT, which bases its decisions on which projects will benefit the entire company most. If there's an impasse, the proposal goes to the CFT steering committee, a smaller and more senior group that includes VPs of IT, supply chain, finance, manufacturing, and marketing. But it's been a long time since the steering committee last had to break a tie.
>
> The CFT reports to the steering committee every six weeks on the overall development budget and where the projects stand, which is good governance. Steering committee meetings also include a discussion of the next ten projects in the queue. We want to make sure we're currently working on the most critical projects, and that the next ten are the most important after those are completed. We have the option of deciding midway through a project to put it aside in favor of something more critical, which is more likely today, given current economic conditions, than previously. But the percentage of projects that are shelved midstream is low. We generally either pick projects with clear returns on investment and short time lines, or very strategic projects, such our new Sappi.com North America Web site, which ties everything we do together with consistent branding.[9]

Sappi has a rich post-implementation harvest process. For larger projects, monthly reviews are conducted for the first year after deployment, with the CFO sitting on the steering committee, and annual reviews from then on. Also, within five years of deployment, internal personnel, often from other parts of the business, conduct an audit (typically three to five people for two weeks). For smaller projects, monthly post-implementation reviews typically end within a year of deployment.

IT is less formally involved in any harvest activity post-deployment. Wittstein says that this is less of a problem when everyone is focused on one large project. But "as we . . . move to many small projects, we will have to improve here," he says.

Wittstein concludes that there are two key success factors for consistently achieving benefits from IT projects: being tough about which projects you accept, and good, old-fashioned project management and execution. "There's nothing more important than execution. Even if you pick the wrong projects, good execution will give you time to recover."

Table 8-2 shows how three enterprises have implemented their virtuous cycles.

Where do we start improving the virtuous cycle?

Because improvement in any part of the virtuous cycle improves value for IT investments, starting anywhere is better than waiting to start in a particular place. Enterprises that practice effective value realization processes can earn as much as 21 percent higher benefits on average than enterprises that do not.

That said, it may be easiest to begin with needs assessment and transparent investment. Most businesses already have investment assessment and decision processes in place, and it represents relatively little change to add IT to the projects that are subject to those criteria and decisions.

TABLE 8-2

Virtuous cycles for Intel, BT, and Sappi

	Intel	BT	Sappi
Planning	Clear business cases, with quantified benefit expectations based on measurable outcomes. Transparent prioritization based on strategic alignment and technical leverage in addition to ROI.	Clear business cases. Exceptions require CEO sign-off. "Hothousing" up front to prototype multiple potential solutions in advance of project start.	Clear business cases, with expected benefits tailored for different types of projects.
Execution	Project phase validation and approval decisions based on established success criteria.	Reduced number of projects to ensure visibility and focus. Projects must deliver every 90 days or face cancellation.	CFT involved in go/no go decisions and as project management office for every project. Frequent status monitoring and validation/prioritization by CFT steering committee and CFT
Harvest	Formal measurement of business benefits based on "clicks" of the value dial. Estimates conducted and managed by finance staff and revisited annually.	Full post-implementation review (PIR) process for all projects. Tied to bonuses and internal learning.	For very large projects, iterative harvesting process beginning immediately after implementation, and continuing for several years afterward. For smaller projects, harvesting completed within one year of implementation.

For most enterprises, improvements in BPR and AD represent refinements, and not massive changes to the way they do business. In that sense, these two elements may represent a path of least resistance. But the biggest payoffs are likely to result from implementing programs to manage enterprise change and manage the harvest. The former, in particular, offers potential for significant advantage over competitors, most of whom have not implemented (and won't in the near future if trends continue) practices and programs to ensure that the enterprise is ready and committed to use new processes and systems when they become available. Further, the CIO can exert considerable influence, if not control, to move the enterprise in this direction, using the project management office as a base for implementing the necessary capabilities. Finally, because executives in general identify a lack of managing organizational change as the biggest obstacle to their initiatives, there's little doubt that movement here will have a significant impact on overall success.

Improvements in the activities of the virtuous cycle will help the CIO make the case for IT as an investment in business performance—to demonstrate the value of IT in unequivocal terms that relate directly to growth and profits. Once the CIO has made the case that every investment in IT creates value for the business, one outcome is certain: recognition of the CIO's value to the enterprise, along with increased opportunities for the CIO and IT. That outcome and those opportunities are the subject of our next chapter.

New
thinking

Value
for
money

New
business
value

Extended
value

[9]

The CIO-plus

If you don't know where you're going,
you'll wind up somewhere else.

—Yogi Berra

INEVITABLY, SUCCESS in your efforts to create and communicate value to your company and your staff produces rewards for you as well as your organization. In this sense, the journey to IT value does not have a final destination. It flows into a world of opportunities for the CIO and the IT team.

As we show later in this chapter, some CIOs, such as Charlie Feld and Bud Mathaisel, have leveraged their CIO experiences into industry leadership and influence as acknowledged gurus of the CIO world. Others have taken paths that have led to senior executive responsibilities outside IT. Marv Adams, formerly CIO of Ford, now manages core financial operations and shared services for financial services giant Fidelity Investments. Guido Sacchi of CompuCredit became the company's VP of corporate strategy and now is a CEO at Moneta Corporation. And Joe

Antonellis of State Street Corporation is now the $7 billion company's vice chairman and head of a major client-services business unit. A decade ago, IT personnel and industry analysts joked that CIO stood for "career is over." But clearly, for successful CIOs, it is anything but.

These CIOs are examples of what we call the *CIO-plus*—simply put, the CIO whose stature and influence inside and outside the enterprise are comparable to those of any other executive. The CIO-plus phenomenon, though long in coming, is not surprising. With the increasing importance of IT to every business, the capabilities and business acumen of the executives responsible for IT inevitably grow as well. Ten years ago, we would have been hard pressed to name a single CIO whose career path had led to the CEO's office. In our research for this book—admittedly, in a sample set of CIOs chosen for proven ability—we encountered three.

The rewards for increased business savvy and credibility flow to everyone in IT. After the IT turnaround at Intel, the IT unit was awarded the challenge of fostering innovation throughout the company—a role no one would have imagined for IT only four years earlier. PMO staff at Solectron routinely leveraged their methods and knowledge of the business to move into business management roles, with the blessing of business unit chiefs and the CIO. Even those who stay in the same IT roles in their companies gain opportunities to identify and implement projects that are far more interesting and valuable than those they could do previously. A rising tide raises all ships.

We have been inspired by the CIOs we interviewed for this book, many of whose careers have risen to new levels of success in the few years since our focused research on this topic began. If their paths are any indication, then CIOs who develop the business acumen necessary to deliver and communicate IT value have exciting futures before them. And IT managers aspiring to greater roles can consider how to build the futures they want on the foundation of their IT expertise.

CIO-plus is attainable

In this chapter, we share stories of highly effective CIOs who took on new business responsibilities, in some cases leaving the office of the CIO entirely. The phenomenon is far from rare. Not every highly capable CIO will find it inevitable (or even necessarily desirable) to make a transition to strictly non-IT responsibilities. But most effective CIOs are already on the way to the expanded responsibilities that characterize the CIO-plus role.

A Gartner Executive Programs survey of about 1,400 CIOs in late 2007 showed that more than half had at least one responsibility outside traditional IT, as shown in figure 9-1. Note in this figure the high proportion of CIOs who have additional responsibilities for the enterprise. Notable are internal roles such as process improvement or facilities, as well as external roles such as enterprise strategy or call center operations. Senior executives apparently recognize these roles as a natural extension of the capabilities that strong CIOs bring to the table.

FIGURE 9-1

More than half of CIOs report having at least one responsibility outside traditional IT

More than three responsibilities	75% Business process improvement 65% Procurement mgmt. 30% Property and facilities 29% Human resources	67% Enterprise strategy planning 38% Customer contact center 41% Innovation office 34% Business development
Two or three responsibilities	60% Business process improvement 32% Procurement provider mgmt. 18% Property and facilities 8% Human resources	32% Enterprise strategy planning 17% Customer contact center 7% Innovation office 8% Business development
Only one responsibility	30% Business process improvement 11% Procurement provider mgmt. 4% Property and facilities	10% Enterprise strategy planning 6% Customer contact center 5% Innovation office

IT

◄———— Internally focused   Externally focused ————►

Source: "Making the Difference: The 2008 CIO Agenda," Gartner EXP Premier Report, January 2008.

Even more significant in potential career mobility, a steadily increasing percentage of CIOs—24 percent as of this writing, up from 15 percent as recently as 2006—are business executives whose first role in IT is CIO. We can assume that for many of these executives, a stint in IT is one among a number of experiences they consider valuable to their careers and is not necessarily the intended end point. But whether or not IT is their final career destination, these nontechnical CIOs change the perception of the role, within and outside their companies, to one that is a respectable—and, at some point, perhaps mandatory—resume entry for an upwardly mobile executive.

The CIO role is a potent launching pad

It doesn't matter whether a business executive became CIO or a CIO gained additional business responsibilities. It doesn't matter whether the new role was a choice or an obligation. What matters is that IT leaders are playing increasingly important roles in the business.

CIOs have every reason to know the plans, strategies, and capabilities of every business unit, because they are charged with automating and informing those strategies. No one in the company, with the possible exception of the COO, knows more about how the company's business processes work than the CIO. And the CIO usually owns the most capable project delivery teams in the enterprise. In short, CIOs are typically associated with the company's best practices for making and executing strategy and delivering services. It's only natural that their enterprises (or others) would call on CIOs when they need capable leaders.

The CIO-plus role does not happen automatically. It takes effort, not only to perform the CIO role well but also to shape the possibilities for doing more. That means making it known that you are interested in an expanded role, seeking opportunities that leverage the CIO experience, and taking on risky new challenges when offered.

Like the CFO, the CIO has legitimate access to every other executive in the company. Before he became CIO of McKesson in 2005, Randy Spratt was a senior non-IT executive. He had full P&L responsibility within McKesson Technology Solutions, whose business is developing, installing, and supporting software applications for the hospital and physician marketplaces. Spratt had some reservations about accepting the CIO role when it was offered: "I was very nervous about going into a role that had no revenue responsibility . . . Revenue hides many sins; the more effective you can be in growing the business, the more room you have to make mistakes. When you're a cost center, you have nothing to go on except year-over-year comparables. But this was clearly important to McKesson's expansion plans. I took it on with the expectation that I'd apply business principles to the role."[1]

Earlier chapters in this book describe how Spratt was able to change the way the IT unit was managed and, with it, the value McKesson gains from its investments in IT. What he didn't expect was how he himself would change as a result of being a CIO: "I didn't aspire to be CIO before I became one. But knowing what I know now, I think I should have. Until you've actually sat in that chair, you don't understand the potential of the position. I'm a much more valuable person to McKesson, and on the American executive scene today, than I was before. The ability to accomplish change that spans the entire business rainbow at McKesson is a lot more interesting than I thought it would be."

Spratt predicts that the role will move soon from a technology focus to one that is oriented to rapid delivery of new products and services—from running the business to growing it. The comparison he makes to marketing is telling, given that a background in marketing is a traditional path to enterprise leadership.

It's not about technologies; it's about strategy and change leadership. In ten to fifteen years a lot of the things that occupy the CIO's time now will look like utilities. You don't worry a lot about where the water and the gas and power come from. In the future we won't worry much about where computer power, storage, connectivity, and software applications come from. The questions will be about how quickly you can deploy those utilities to bring new products and service to market. The role will have a lot of the speed and risk elements you associate with marketing—how fast can we deploy, as opposed to how do we build a risk-free data center?

Oh, the places you'll go

Figure 9-2 summarizes the most prominent CIO-plus career paths we have seen in our research. Each role depicted in this figure has elements of business and IT responsibilities, with some weighted more heavily to one end or another. As we've shown so far, effective CIOs are more than technical leaders. They describe their value in business terms, and they sign up for and deliver business change. That's why we drew the CIO role higher on the business scale than an IT manager's role.

FIGURE 9-2

CIO-plus career paths

But where do CIOs go from there? Some opt to stay in the CIO role, doing it ever more effectively and loving every day of it. Others choose to move to new CIO roles, often outside their companies, or become CIO consultants, sharing their experience through publications, speaking opportunities, and other externally oriented forums. These are the CIO gurus whom we often see in the press. Our conversations with CIOs playing this role show that they are motivated not only by the freedom and rewards of the role but also by a desire to share their hard-won knowledge of what it takes to succeed with others—to give back to the profession.

Many CIOs are moving upward on the chart, gaining additional business responsibilities while retaining their CIO duties. These *extended CIOs* are in essence doing two or three jobs, in some cases as a more or less explicit test of their capabilities. Other CIOs, however, relinquish their technical responsibilities as they take on more explicitly nontechnical business roles. These newly minted CxOs may have their successors in the CIO role reporting to them, or they may have no direct responsibility for IT.

Note that there is no value judgment implied by the CIO's location in this two-dimensional picture. The upper-right corner may be the busiest, because it implies heavy responsibilities both in IT and elsewhere in the business. There's a limit to how many full-time jobs anyone can handle at once, and CIOs who move into the upper-left corner zone occupied by non-IT CxOs inevitably relinquish all or most of their IT responsibilities. These CIOs often start by moving "up" into the CIO-plus role and then take emerging opportunities to move leftward into other roles. But others, especially those who came to the CIO role from a non-IT business role, sometimes make the jump in one step.

Furthermore, continuing in a CIO role does not in any way represent underachieving. Many CIOs we interviewed were highly satisfied executives. The role emphasized skills they possessed, they had significant standing to influence important changes in their businesses, and they felt their contributions were both valuable and well recognized. As one CIO said, "I'm very good at this. Why would I move to a role that required a totally different set of skills?"

In the rest of this chapter we tell the stories of CIOs who have followed their own paths to greater responsibility. Then we discuss considerations for the next step on your trajectory. We repeat that these stories inspire us. We expect that they will inspire many current and future CIOs as well, including (we hope) some who may not have previously imagined or coveted a CIO entry on their resumes.

CIO and loving it

Some CIOs love being CIO. They find enormous challenge and satisfaction in creating a world-class IT organization—one that runs smoothly and efficiently while providing the agility the organization needs—and building world-class business involvement and oversight for the IT function. For many people, especially engineers, the role of CIO is simply delightful. They can continually seek challenges to solve and opportunities to create, working with IT staff and business colleagues to bring them to fruition. Continually increasing integration into the strategic decision making of the organization allows these CIOs and their staffs to take on increasingly interesting challenges.

The CIO who loves it often stays with her company for long periods, helping it grow and growing with it. Or she may move to a CIO role in a larger or more IT-intensive company in order to take on the challenge and gain the rewards of managing a larger organization. Some attain CIO guru status, where they can pass on what they have learned. But many more are content being CIO "for now," considering their next roles as opportunities arise.

When DirectEnergy, the North American subsidiary of U.K. energy company Centrica PLC, was preparing for its next stage of growth, the senior team wanted a very specific kind of CIO—one with telecom experience who'd also worked on Wall Street. The Wall Street experience would help in understanding the company's energy trading business and in navigating a series of acquisitions. Telecom experience would help in understanding the firm's regulated markets as well as the importance of keeping a large customer-service infrastructure running reliably. The management team doubted that anyone was available with that blend of experience, but the job description was tailor-made for Kumud Kalia, who had worked for Dresdner on Wall Street and Qwest Communications in Colorado.

As a member of the company's senior executive team from the start, Kalia sees his role as more than just managing technology. The company is growing fast, and acquisition is a major part of that growth. Every acquisition brings a complex legacy of multiple partially integrated applications and different ways of doing similar business processes. Kalia built a team of process engineers to help his colleagues understand the opportunities and importance of improving the firm's processes, not just automating their requirements. And he continually helps them understand why they must not operate their merged companies completely independently—that there are synergies to be attained by leveraging internal best practices across multiple internal companies.

As the company's top IT executive, Kalia is a respected and influential partner to the other business executives of the firm. He and his team deliver on requirements, and his suggestions for improving the business are listened to. He has helped to improve efficiencies and customer service across a rapidly growing company. Kalia doesn't know what his next role will be. But he's finding his job as CIO in a fast-growing company to be both challenging and rewarding.

Sam Coursen does know what his role should be. When asked to complete the sentence, "If I weren't a CIO I'd be . . .," he simply said, "I love being a CIO."[2] A longtime employee of AT&T and its acquired firm NCR, Coursen became NCR's CIO in 1998. During seven years as CIO, he and his team helped NCR achieve world-class cost efficiencies through process reengineering, consolidation, automation, and outsourcing. As soon as he announced his retirement, at age fifty-five, recruiters began to call.

"Freescale Semiconductor had just spun out from Motorola, and they were reinvigorating the senior management team," Coursen says. "Freescale needed an IT transformation similar to the one I implemented at NCR." In the years since, Coursen has helped to transform the way Freescale IT works, showing the value the unit delivers and demonstrating how effective use of new IT can help the company to grow.

It's unclear what Coursen will do after his IT transformation is complete at Freescale. But it's a good bet that IT will be a large component of the role. And it's likely that part of the role will be publicizing what he has learned about how to manage IT, because Coursen wants to give back to the profession. "Everything I do in terms of creating and conveying value for IT, I learned from someone else . . . So I'm into best-practice sharing. I can't just hoard all the knowledge for myself."

The CIO Guru

The desire to share the best practices he's learned and developed is often the first step to CIO gurudom—leveraging the CIO's experience to generate value as an advisor too. Bud Mathaisel is a serial CIO, having played the role in industry-leading companies such as Disney, Ford, and Solectron. He was also founding director of Ernst & Young's Center for Business Innovation in Boston. After leaving his prior role as CIO and chief process officer at Solectron, he became CIO and chief operating officer–North America and Europe at Achievo, a firm that provides China-based offshore services to a global set of clients. Like other CIO gurus, Mathaisel has served on numerous advisory boards and boards of directors, and written articles for the trade press. Whether his success stems from his MIT education or from other factors, he has won numerous awards from trade magazines and associations, including being named to InfoWorld's list of the top 25 CTOs in 2008.[3]

Charlie Feld's career is instructive for IT managers aspiring to the CIO guru role. Originally a systems engineer with IBM, Feld became CIO for one of his clients, Frito-Lay, in 1981. At Frito-Lay he led the development of an integrated computer system to connect all departments in a common communications and data network—the foundation for a high-velocity distribution system and a handheld computer network for ten thousand salespeople, which earned the company world renown.

In 1992, Feld leveraged the numerous awards he and his unit had received to create The Feld Group, a team of IT executives who took temporary positions as turnaround CIOs for their clients. Feld himself served as senior vice president and CIO at Burlington Northern, managing the massive integration of the Burlington Northern and Santa Fe railroad companies. Then he took on the challenge of transforming Delta Air Lines' entire IT foundation in advance of Y2K and the Internet age. He moved from the CIO role to be Delta's "e-leader" responsible for dozens of initiatives that improved how the airline relates to customers, business partners, and employees, and then he became acting CIO of First Data Resources (FDR), a division of First Data Corp. In 2003, when global IT services provider EDS purchased The Feld Group, Feld began playing numerous roles in the company. After the closing of the EDS/HP merger in October 2008, Feld retired from EDS and went back out on his own as a noted consultant, speaker, and founder of the Center for IT Leadership.[4]

The guru role takes more than being a good manager. Gaining recognition as a CIO guru requires actively promoting the work one has done. Over the past fifteen years, Feld has been cited regularly as one of the world's top IT leaders by magazines and industry organizations. He has also written numerous articles for, and has been profiled in, management publications such as *Harvard Business Review, CIO,* and *Computerworld.* Feld is not alone in this regard. Sam Coursen has appeared in numerous publications, and Intel's IT leaders actively promote the techniques and results they have built. Such self-promotion is essential to the recognition and impact that are required of a CIO who wants to influence other CIOs.

As Feld's background shows, the CIO guru role is a risky and demanding one that is not for the weak of heart. The guru is often called on to solve complex IT-related business problems whose resolution is critical to the businesses involved. On the other hand, if your early CIO roles provide you with experience, lever-ageable results, and enough wealth to ensure the independence of your opinions, you may have a shot at the guru role.

The Extended CIO

The extended CIO role is often the CIO's first foray into non-IT roles. The title is typically something like "senior vice president and CIO"—a title that reflects both the holder's primary focus on IT and the additional responsibilities that management has assigned.

The extended CIO often takes on responsibility for functions or tasks that are related to the CIO role and do not require a full CxO-level role. These may be temporary assignments (such as merger integration) or ongoing responsibility for centralized ser-vices that can be managed as infrastructure (such as facilities or physical security). Other CIOs take responsibility for areas that are not usually managed by a seniormost executive, such as busi-ness processes or strategy.

The extended CIO role can be a career aspiration for many IT executives who love the challenges of the CIO role but who want the expanded influence on the business that goes with additional corporate responsibilities. The role offers the CIO greater influ-ence on the business as a whole and often helps the CIO transition to a non-IT C-level executive role. It is also a natural progression for IT executives who are comfortable speaking the language of business value.

Common to all extended CIO roles is that the executive's pri-mary role is CIO. Other responsibilities are usually additional and not primary. Also common to the role is that the new respon-sibilities are seen as either the next step to a higher business role or an additional set of duties the CIO sought. As noted, most CIOs are already in this role to some extent.

Sometimes the extended CIO role is temporary, although the temporary role may be repeated or indefinitely extended. In 2006, McKesson's Randy Spratt was asked to manage the integration of an acquired firm, Per Se! Technologies. From the start, he was interested in the project for its potential to provide a template for McKesson's approach to integrating acquisitions.

> I discovered that we had approached every acquisition as a case unto itself. The things you needed to capture and deliver for business integration were left to the individuals who did the job, usually high-potential individuals. It was also usually the first and last time they did such a project, so there was no corporate learning. So we set up a little office of M&A integration that manages the integration of acquisitions, and it's produced a really great business integration capability— checklists, project plans, toolkits, methodologies to set up a business integration team. This has added to the view that the IT organization can think in terms of business results and outcomes.[5]

Spratt has leveraged the credibility he developed for the central IT organization since 2005 to transform IT operations throughout McKesson. In 2008, he and McKesson's divisional CIOs agreed to embark on McKesson's first-ever companywide IT strategy. "We've got the infrastructure consolidation in process, so what remains is how IT is serving the business needs of the company, and the leverage we can get for that. So rather than talk about what it costs to replace seventeen general ledger systems, we have to talk about what it costs the business to run seventeen different finance processes, and take it up to the business process reengineering level. That will take us to the next level of operational efficiencies and tie us directly to the performance of the business and its expansion strategies."

That systematic approach to managing IT's impact on business performance is now standard operating procedure for merger integration at McKesson. Spratt says, "Instead of leaving them to drift on their own where we do not have a singular strategy— for ERP or sales support, for example—we have a lens to look at them."

Some CIOs find that extended duties become permanent and welcome additions to their roles. Butch Leonardson is CIO of Boeing Employees Credit Union (BECU). Credit unions, even large ones such as BECU, thrive through customer intimacy and customer service. In his role as CIO, Leonardson has constantly worked to remind his IT staff of that fact. "IT needs to know all the moments of truth with our customers, and make them incredibly exciting," he says. "You have to be a student of the business. IT planners become business planners, part of the business conversation. Then the whole idea of an IT strategy doesn't disappear; it fades into the tapestry of the enterprise's strategic plan. 'Here's our strategic encounter with the customer, and IT is a thread in the tapestry.' "[6]

Since 2006, Leonardson has cochaired a BECU customer and employee loyalty initiative called Net Promoter.[7] In this role, he is constantly examining ways to measure and improve customer service. By measuring how specific types of interactions affect specific dimensions of customer satisfaction, he and his colleagues can design process changes, information provision, and specific interventions to improve it. "When a BECU employee logs on in the morning, if he's [customer-facing] staff, he sees our four strategic objectives—the target and where we are," Leonardson explains. "With Net Promoter we're supposed to be at 73.5 percent right now, and we're at 74.6 percent." This means that a net of nearly 75 percent of customers would recommend BECU to friends, family, or colleagues.

Leonardson continues to seek improvements in the company's ability to use data to improve performance for customer service. He and his staff are now working with an outside firm to benchmark Net Promoter scores against those of other firms and to take the net promoter metrics down from the overall company to the branch level.

The customer experience role translates to Leonardson's dealings with colleagues. For example, he is trying to change the way he talks with the board and how board members think of IT's role. "I believe that boards can evolve, and they need to see IT spend not as IT spend but as customer value spend. I always present to the board from the member perspective, not the IT perspective. One branch manager told me that the stuff we rolled out changed his life."

CIO guru Bud Mathaisel has played the role of extended CIO at two companies. At Solectron, in addition to his CIO role, Mathaisel was chief process officer, responsible for ensuring that business processes were well designed and that everything possible was done to constantly improve them. In the process role, Mathaisel regularly spent time with customers, seeking ways to make Solectron easier to do business with. He also spent time internally ensuring that the firm's processes were functioning effectively.

Although responsible for processes, Mathaisel was primarily still the company's CIO. He strove to make IT a focal point for excellent practices that the firm could use elsewhere. For example, his PMO became so highly regarded that business units regularly poached PMO staff to manage projects in their units. Mathaisel felt that was an honor. He could train new PMO managers. But the credibility he gained through excellent processes and people could not be built overnight. He leveraged the performance of his IT unit to improve the performance of Solectron, his own ability to change business processes, and his own personal credibility inside and outside the company. Recently Mathaisel left Solectron for another extended CIO role—CIO and chief operating officer at Achievo, an outsourcing business that leverages its application development offices in China across a network of offices in the rest of the world.[8]

Guido Sacchi, formerly of CompuCredit, extended the CIO role all the way to the CEO's office at Moneta Corporation. While still a CIO, he described this as a natural next step for many CIOs as the roles converge. "For me, the IT role has changed a lot in the last eighteen months. I'm now seen as a business person, a C-level executive who's in charge of IT," he told us in 2008. "But the debate is much livelier about how we make the business better. I'm focused a lot more on information, a lot less on technology. Our intellectually challenging problems are around information flows and decision making. Some of our most successful projects recently are about BI, or what we call the 'data supply chain'—asking ourselves, 'What kinds of decisions do the leaders make on a daily basis, and how we can improve that dramatically?' "[9]

Beginning in 2006, Sacchi served CompuCredit as CIO and vice president of corporate strategy. He set up a corporate process for innovation management, with an emphasis on funding and launching new business as well as enterprisewide change initiatives. The role gave him plenty of opportunities to talk about enterprisewide business change with executives throughout the organization. For example, he launched an initiative called Operational Leverage to dramatically improve operational efficiencies in traditional overhead areas such as IT infrastructure, telephony, and call center footprint.

In 2008 Sacchi was asked to serve as acting COO of one of CompuCredit's IT-intensive new businesses, a mobile phone venture that has a large credit component. In his words, "I'm fortunate enough to have been offered the opportunity to try my hand at a C-level business role with P&L responsibility. It's definitely of interest to me . . . I'll try it and see if I can be successful at it. I've been a CIO here for almost six years, and it's probably time to let someone else grow into that role. We have a great team and a clear succession plan, and it's time to give someone else a chance." Sacchi's move to the CEO role at Moneta Corporation shows that there are indeed multiple options for the CIO-plus.

The CxO with IT

Some CIOs, in extending their roles, find that their business responsibilities require even more attention than their IT roles. These leaders, who typically have titles like executive vice president or chief (anything) officer, still have IT among their responsibilities. But it is a smaller component of their portfolios than it is for the extended CIO. These people—whether chief administrative officer (CAO), chief operating officer (COO), executive vice president of shared services, or another title—are CxOs with IT.

In practice, the extended CIO and the CxO with IT share many similar characteristics, responsibilities, challenges, and rewards. Their business responsibilities may be of similar types, but one has more of them than the other. There is, however, a clear distinction. The extended CIO is still CIO. The CxO with IT retains a large component of IT in her portfolio but hires a new CIO to manage the IT function.

In the 1990s, Marv Adams was executive vice president and CIO at Bank One Corporation, having previously served in engineering and management roles at IBM and then Xerox. BankOne was highly IT-intensive and Marv learned a lot about managing IT from the experience.

In 2000, Adams was named CIO at Ford Motor Company. In that role, he was responsible for overseeing the company's worldwide IT strategy, development, and infrastructure while focusing on making Ford more efficient and effective in that area of the business. In May 2005, he took on the additional role of senior vice president of corporate strategy. In that capacity, he led not only IT strategy but automotive and company strategy, helping Ford chart its course through major business changes in a world of globalization while retaining his CIO responsibilities.

He left Ford in 2006 to become CIO of Citigroup. At Citigroup, he was responsible for the global leadership of corporate infrastructure and systems. He was a member of the Citigroup Management Committee. He also led the firm's CIO Council, with responsibility for the company's enterprise IT direction.

Adams is now president of Fidelity Shared Services, a 12,000-person organization providing shared services to other units within global financial provider Fidelity Investments. The newly formed organization consists of three units, each with its own president. Fidelity Technology Group manages IT services, including infrastructure, applications, and Web sites, for both customer-facing and internally focused activities. Fidelity Enterprise Operations includes core financial services processing such as pricing and cash management, other operations such as supply management, and a set of shared services based in India. Fidelity Real Estate Company provides real estate planning and services to other units in the global enterprise. Adams is no longer an IT executive; he's a business executive to whom the leaders of IT and others services report.

Providing shared services is an interesting challenge for a firm like Fidelity, whose divisions pride themselves on their independence. A key part of Adams's role will be to transform structures and deliver effective services to a diverse set of business units across the company. A major challenge will be to help change the firm's culture to show that using common services can be useful, even for highly independent business units. He and his senior executive peers believe that his experience, both inside and outside of financial services, will help Adams and his team to lead the transformation successfully.[10]

The Non-IT CxO

IT is the lifeblood of some businesses. CIOs who can make the connection between IT's mission and the business's success, and who can speak the language of business—starting with the P&L—can in some cases move to the corner office as head of a company division, a spin-off, or a start-up. We appreciate that it is still relatively rare for CIOs to make that jump; even now, rather few businesses think of IT capability in the same terms that they think of sales or manufacturing. But we see evidence that this is changing.

Doug Busch was an engineering manager at Intel when he was tapped to be CIO shortly after the April Fools' incident, as we described earlier. Busch took over an IT unit that was truly an example of the cobbler's children wearing no shoes. The IT unit of Intel— the firm that powered the IT units of the world—was suffering from poor service and lack of respect from the business. Busch and his team turned around the perception by implementing strong oversight and improvement practices. They improved reliability, improved service to internal customers, and experienced a steady increase in the number of Intel employees who called IT a partner. And they did this while continuously reducing the IT budget. Building on the success in improving IT's services and costs, Busch and his staff launched an effort to improve the innovativeness of his unit and the company as a whole. The effort led to more than $400 million in improvements from 2004 to 2007.

After leading the successful transformation of the IT unit, Busch was tapped to become chief technology officer of Intel's Digital Health Group. The new unit, focused on medical applications of Intel technology, is completely separate from IT. Busch, no longer CIO, is now on the other side, asking his former IT colleagues to help him deliver on commitments.

Joe Antonellis of State Street Corporation has spent his whole professional life in banking, and all in the Boston area. After an operational management role at Bank of Boston, he moved to financial services firm State Street to lead a business unit that was focused on high-throughput transaction processing. In 2002, State Street's CEO asked Joe to become CIO. Although he had no technical experience, he understood how the company's processes were enabled by IT. He understood the limits of IT in the company, and, most important, he knew the senior team well enough to be able to tune IT's services and processes to make them easier to deal with. He also had a keen understanding of State Street's customers' IT needs and how best to deliver against current and future market developments. By the time Antonellis took over IT, it was well managed technically and was making improvements in governance and application development, but it had some cost issues. Antonellis took on some tough challenges that needed strong senior support: changing the application development process, changing the IT funding process, opening offshore development offices, introducing technology innovations, and reducing costs.

The work paid off for the company and for Antonellis. After three years, he was asked to take on operations responsibility for the firm's biggest division in addition to his IT role. In 2006, he was appointed vice chairman with additional responsibility as head of Investor Services in North America and global investment manager outsourcing services. In 2008 he hired his replacement in the CIO role, allowing Antonellis to focus more fully on his clients and his corporate leadership responsibilities.

Charting your course

If you're a CIO, you should start planning your next step now. If you're an IT manager, plan how to gain the experience you need. Do you want to move into the CIO role? Or move to a business role and consider moving to CIO or CIO-plus later? And if you're a businessperson considering a CIO position, congratulations on your foresight.

Where you can go depends on what you enjoy, what you're good at, what you can improve through new experiences, and what your company needs. These factors don't always come together to make you a CIO-plus, or they may not come together in your current company. But as our stories show, they cannot come together if you do not perform your role well; and if you perform your role well, additional opportunities are likely.

To increase your chances, take steps now to plot a course. Start by understanding what roles may be possible for you (as shown in table 9-1). Consider the descriptions and ask whether your experiences and interests are a good fit for these positions. Keep in mind that there are plenty of rewards and challenges available to successful CIOs, and plenty of opportunities to take on wider responsibilities in the business without changing jobs.

We've seen examples of CIOs doing all these roles (and shared the stories of many of them). But people are not interchangeable. So consider whether the role is something you'd like and would be good at with practice and experience.

Next, start planning a path in the business/technology responsibility map. The CIOs we profiled in this chapter took a variety of paths. Note that none of the career paths was completely planned. You can't dictate the future, but you can take steps to improve the chances that your future will be what you want. Each of the people asked for, or accepted, a role because it was important for him or for the company. Then they added to their credibility and options through a combination of planned action and unplanned opportunities. But they all built on their skills and interests to do more than they had been doing before. And they all proactively reached out to do something more than they were originally doing.

TABLE 9-1

Potential CIO-plus roles

CxO role	What to leverage into the role	Obstacles to overcome
CAO—chief administrative officer (related roles: head of shared services) Typically responsible for HR, facilities, and other administrative functions delivered to the lines of business.	Extensive elements of administration are already included in the CIO's responsibilities. Can leverage abilities to deliver infrastructure services and process changes to improve performance and cost of the administrative functions.	Natural extension of CIO role. But, if merging silos into shared services, expect significant political and organizational change obstacles. If necessary, find eager early adopters and then slowly ramp up pressure on late adopters.
CSO—chief strategy officer Responsible for developing corporate and often product strategy for the company.	CIO's knowledge of corporate strategy, process, and capabilities is often among the strongest in the company. CIO already has relationships to other executives for both formal and informal discussions.	Refocus from an execution mind-set to a strategic one, including new language and skills.
CFO—chief financial officer Provides financial management and information to the enterprise.	Financial components of the CIO's responsibilities: benefits management and delivery, and oversight of a significant budget can be viewed as representing P&L experience.	The thinking style of a CFO is the same as that of a CIO: analytical; must demonstrate a bias for action; must either get the appropriate educational credentials or be supported by a controller.
COO—chief operating officer Responsible for executing and improving the operational processes of the company.	Technology is embedded throughout the operations of the organization; leverage the process view of the organization; optimize the organization.	Demonstrate the ability to look across the organization from process and operational perspectives.
CEO—chief executive officer In charge of the total management of a corporation, organization, or agency.	Strategy; transformational delivery; process view of operations.	Need to pull the entire package together: MBA, strategic thinking, sales and marketing.

But remember always that blind ambition is neither useful nor pretty. Every one of the CIO-plus people we interviewed found that they gained their extended roles through collaboration and helping others succeed, and not through political wheeling and dealing. In most cases, they were asked to take on extended roles, either by the company's senior leaders or the leaders of other firms. And when they did push for an extended role, they gained the role not through politics but through their knowledge, credibility, relationships, and hard work. No executive wants to work with someone who is maneuvering to take his job. But nearly every executive, when looking to fill an open position, will reach out to trusted colleagues who have helped him (or others) be successful in the past.

In this book, we've described the path to becoming that trusted colleague—the one who can be relied on to deliver value. Our final chapter is a summary of the key messages in this book.

New
thinking

Value
for
money

New
business
value

Extended
value

[10]

There's Never Been a Better Time to Be a CIO

There has never been a better time for a capable executive to take on the role of CIO. We would not be surprised to see executives on the CEO track make a point of adding the CIO role to their resumes, just as previous generations of ambitious executives sought stints in product management and marketing.

We hope that this book will help you make your business and yourself more capable and effective managers of IT. We are certain that if you do, there will be more than enough success to go around, no matter where the role of CIO leads.

The CIO-plus role is the reward at the end of a long journey. It starts with years of remembering that it's not about IT but about business performance, because business performance is the language of IT value. Establish value for money, show how IT is an investment in future business performance, implement the virtuous cycle, keep score—and watch what happens. By remembering that it's all about the business, you inevitably bring favorable attention to yourself. If you show you can provide value, value will come back to you. And everyone will gain in the process.

The CIO who follows the path laid out in this book is sure to increase perception of IT value in the rest of the business and improve opportunities for herself and the rest of the IT team. We know this because we have seen it repeatedly. In short, it's worth the effort. We close with a brief summary of the main points.

Remember: It's all about business performance

- Before you change anything else, change what you think and say, and always focus your comments on business outcomes.

- Recognize those IT management concepts and practices that once seemed useful but in reality are value traps.

- Blow your own horn by measuring and expressing IT value in terms that are visible to, and meaningful to, the rest of the business.

- Instead of talking about what the machines do, talk about what the business does and explain how IT can help it do more and better.

- Use the head-of-sales rule: if the head of sales wouldn't say it that way, neither should you.

Show value for money

- The inescapable table stakes for communicating IT value are to show conclusively that IT delivers the right services, at the right level of quality, at the right price.

- Measure and communicate unit costs and quality in terms that refer to services that touch the rest of the business.

- Players know the score. Benchmark your performance against yourself and against external peers.

- Provide information that will help everyone in the business manage consumption of IT services and so reduce costs.

Show the value of IT as an investment in business performance

- Do everything you can to improve the enterprise's execution of the virtuous cycle: needs identification, transparent investment, business process redesign, organizational change, application development, and harvesting of returns.

- Help the business focus on strategy, processes, and operational performance measures, all of which will clarify which opportunities matter most.

- Consider opportunities to use IT to inform internal and external audiences, to optimize processes, and to reshape your interactions with customers and suppliers.

- Assess the potential of projects to contribute to the most important business outcomes. Use the P&L to measure hard benefits, and use operational metrics to measure soft benefits when possible.

- When you invest in IT, use a structured process with clear roles and responsibilities.

- Improve application development, business process redesign, and especially management of organizational change. Everyone knows that managing change is a problem, but few organizations make the effort to address it.

- When an initiative is completed, measure to make sure the benefits promised up front are delivered, and use what you learn by measuring to improve up-front estimates and the investment process.

TABLE 10-1

Focus changes as value delivery matures

Value trap	The new reality	Value for money	IT as investment in new business value
We shouldn't have to talk about our performance; it speaks for itself.	People only see what affects them most, and that's usually the problems.	Talk about performance of the IT function in business terms.	Talk about improved business performance resulting from IT's involvement.
IT is a cost of doing business.	If IT is just a cost, then it's something to be constantly reduced.	Show how your organization delivers the right services at the right cost and quality levels.	Plan for specific types of business value return from each investment, and then use disciplined harvest processes to assess and report the value delivered.
IT managers deliver great technology for the enterprise.	Technology is not an outcome. It sets up CIOs to get credit for cost and trouble, but not for value.	Focus on delivering great IT services, not great technologies.	Focus on delivering business change enabled by technology.
Nothing is perfect (especially anything as complex as IT).	If IT fails when the chips are down, IT can't be trusted. If we don't discuss how much failure is too much, then it's always too much. And if we don't take a customer focus on recovery, then every failure creates animosity.	Show that you know where your service is great and where it's not, and that you're making the stuff that's not great better all the time. Strive for graceful, customer-focused recovery from service failures.	Build excellent project management to reduce the likelihood and impact of project failures and to give effective early warning.
If you don't follow our rules, we can't guarantee it'll work.	Focusing on rules instead of reasons doesn't make IT look helpful. If business leaders can't see the rationale for the rules, then IT is an obstruction.	Explain the reasons for standards, but have customer-focused ways to evaluate exceptions and potential changes to standards.	Show how changing the "rules" (such as standardizing business processes or extending them to customers) may improve the way the business works.
"The business" is IT's customer.	IT should be a peer, not just a vendor.	Focus on effective collaboration with people throughout the business.	Make IT leaders and concepts essential parts of all major business decisions.
The customer is always right.	Business executives need business change, not specific technologies. And they don't often want to pay for important capabilities that don't have direct payoff to their units' plans.	Refocus discussions to the price and quality of services being supplied, not the specifics of how they are delivered. Use information to change arguments into trade-offs.	Focus on the business outcome needed, and then work with business colleagues to identify and evaluate potential options.

Earlier in this book we discussed how value traps blind IT professionals and the rest of the business to the value created and delivered by IT. Table 10-1 shows a revised version of the value traps table presented in chapter 2, this time with brief pointers on how to handle the value traps in terms of value for money and IT as an investment in business performance—two key steps on the path to IT value.

The end of this path leads to the CIO-plus organization, where options for the professionals who work in IT are more numerous and exciting than ever before in the history of the profession. Ten years ago, we would have been hard pressed to find a single CIO who had become a CEO. That ambition is no longer hard to believe; we have seen it achieved more than once, and with increasing frequency. Indeed, we believe that ambitious executives in every discipline will increasingly make it a point to add a tour of duty as CIO to their resumes.

IT has become indispensable to every business of any size. The inevitable result is the increasing importance of showing value. A small but growing group of CIOs has figured out how to show value and deliver increasing value in terms that are utterly convincing to their enterprises. There is no reason that any CIO cannot follow their example. We wish you every success in doing so, and we hope this book will be a useful guide to you on the way.

NOTES

Chapter 1

1. Intel's IT unit used this incident to dramatically improve the value it provides to the business, as we show later in this book.

2. M. Curley, "The IT Transformation at Intel," *MIS Quarterly Executive* 5, no. 4 (December 2006): 155–168; G. Westerman and M. Curley, "Building IT-Enabled Innovation Capabilities at Intel," *MIS Quarterly Executive* 7, no. 1 (March 2008): 33–48; additional interviews with Intel IT managers conducted by George Westerman.

3. Artifacts that developed following the Intel IT transformation became part of a new framework called the IT Capability Maturity Framework, which is being codeveloped by the Innovation Value Institute Consortium (http://ivi.nuim.ie/).

4. Cara Schnaper interview conducted by Richard Hunter and George Westerman, February 19, 2009.

5. Donna Scott, "The High Cost of Achieving Higher Levels of Availability," Gartner Research Note SPA-13-9852, June 29, 2001.

6. Butch Leonardson interview conducted by Richard Hunter, June 10, 2008.

7. Bud Mathaisel interview conducted by George Westerman and Peter Weill, Cambridge, MA, May 19, 2005. Included in George Westerman, Peter Weill, Chris Foglia, and Nils Fonstad, "Building and Maintaining Credibility: Experienced CIOs Comment," video, MIT Sloan Center for Information Systems Research, 2005.

8. Guido Sacchi interview conducted by Richard Hunter, December 20, 2006.

Chapter 2

1. Ken Venner interview conducted by Richard Hunter, July 16, 2008.

2. G. Westerman and P. Weill, "What Makes CIOs Effective: The Perspective of Non-IT Executives," *MIT Sloan CISR Research Briefings* V, 2C (July 2005).

3. M. Smith and K. Potter, "IT Spending and Staffing Report, 2009," Gartner Research Note G00164940, January 27, 2009.

4. As described in R. Hunter, A. Apfel, K. Mcgee, R. Handler, M. Smith, and W. Maurer, "A Simple Framework to Translate IT Benefits into Business Value Impact," Gartner Research Note G00156986, May 16, 2008.

5. MIT Sloan CISR Survey of 1,508 IT leaders conducted in 2007.

6. Robert Proulx interview conducted by Richard Hunter, March 31, 2005.

7. Butch Leonardson interview conducted by Richard Hunter, June 10, 2008.

8. Westerman and Weill, "What Makes CIOs Effective."

9. Cara Schnaper interview conducted by Richard Hunter and George Westerman, February 19, 2009.

10. D. Flint, "The User's View of Why IT Projects Fail," Gartner Research Note G00124846, February 4, 2005.

11. Trey Lewis interview conducted by Richard Hunter, September 9, 2008.

12. John Hammergren interview conducted by Richard Hunter, December 6, 2006.

13. Standish Group, "The CHAOS Report (1994)," http://www.standishgroup.com/sample_research/chaos_1994_1.php.

14. Lars Mieritz, "Exploring the Relationship Between Project Size and Success," Gartner Research Note G00155650, March 4, 2008.

15. "Making the Difference: The 2008 CIO Agenda," Gartner Executive Programs Premier Report, January 2008.

16. See, for example, James Heskett, Earl Sasser, and Leonard Schlesinger, *The Service Profit Chain: How Leading Companies Link Profit and Growth to Loyalty, Satisfaction, and Value* (New York: Free Press, 1997).

17. G. Westerman and R. Hunter, *IT Risk: Turning Business Threats into Competitive Advantage* (Boston: Harvard Business School Press, 2007), shows that effective risk management does more than reduce the number of incidents. It also allows IT and business executives to have more-effective conversations about IT management in general. IT risk management capability is built on three core disciplines: a well-structured, well-managed IT foundation; a risk-aware culture that is able to discuss and make trade-offs about risks; and a thorough but not overly bureaucratic risk governance process to gain information about risks and ensure that they are being addressed appropriately.

18. Al-Noor Ramji interview conducted by George Westerman, Peter Weill, and Nils Fonstad, Cambridge, MA, March 15, 2005. Included in Peter Weill, George Westerman, Chris Foglia, and Nils Fonstad, "Achieving Effective IT Oversight: Experienced CIOs Comment," video, MIT Sloan Center for Information Systems Research, 2005.

19. Guido Sacchi interview conducted by Richard Hunter, December 20, 2006.

20. Westerman and Hunter, *IT Risk*, 4–5.

21. Al-Noor interview, 2005.

22. Sam Coursen interview conducted by Richard Hunter, July 29, 2008.

Chapter 3

1. Guido Sacchi interview conducted by Richard Hunter, December 20, 2006.

2. Cynthia Beath and Jeanne Ross, "JM Family Enterprises Inc.: Selectively Outsourcing for Increased Business Value," MIT Center for Information Systems Research Working Paper #358, April 2006; additional discussions with JM Family executives conducted by George Westerman and Peter Weill in 2006 and 2009.

3. Karl Wachs interview conducted by George Westerman, Dallas, TX, March 7, 2005. Included in Peter Weill, George Westerman, Chris Foglia, and Nils Fonstad, "Achieving Effective IT Oversight: Experienced CIOs Comment," video, MIT Sloan Center for Information Systems Research, 2005.

4. Kevin Vasconi interview conducted by Richard Hunter, December 11, 2006.

5. Randy Spratt interview conducted by Richard Hunter, July 25, 2008.

6. Ibid.

7. Daniel Janeba interview conducted by Richard Hunter, October 23, 2008.

8. Randy Spratt interview, 2008.

9. M. Curley, "The IT Transformation at Intel," *MIS Quarterly Executive* 5, no. 4 (December 2006): 155–168; G. Westerman and M. Curley, "Building IT-enabled Innovation Capabilities at Intel," *MIS Quarterly Executive* 7, no. 1 (March 2008): 33–48; additional interviews with Intel IT managers conducted by George Westerman.

10. Sam Coursen interview conducted by Richard Hunter, July 29, 2008.

11. Peter Bennington interview conducted by Richard Hunter, October 7, 2008.

12. Sam Coursen interview, 2008. See also D. Marchand, W. Kettinger, and J. D. Rollins, *Information Orientation: The Link to Business* (New York: Oxford University Press, 2001).

13. Cara Schnaper interview conducted by Richard Hunter and George Westerman, February 19, 2009.

14. Randy Spratt interview, 2008.

15. Cynthia Beath and Jeanne Ross, "JM Family Enterprises Inc: Selectively Outsourcing for Increased Business Value," MIT Center for Information Systems Research Working Paper #358, April 2006, plus additional discussions with JM Family executives conducted by George Westerman and Peter Weill in 2006 and 2009.

16. Donna Scott, "The High Cost of Achieving Higher Levels of Availability," Gartner Research Note SPA-13-9852, June 29, 2001.

17. Based on engagement conducted by Richard Hunter and Graham Waller, Gartner, July 11, 2008.

18. Randy Spratt interview, 2008.

Chapter 4

1. The non-IT executives rated business value from IT (BVIT) using an eight-item scale which MIT CISR has validated in repeated studies. BVIT is statistically significantly correlated with industry-adjusted measures of financial performance in publicly-traded companies.

2. Butch Leonardson interview conducted by Richard Hunter, June 10, 2008.

3. Bud Mathaisel interview conducted by George Westerman and Peter Weill, Cambridge, MA, May 19, 2005. Included in George Westerman, Peter Weill, Chris Foglia, Nils Fonstad, "Communicating with Business Executives: Experienced CIOs Comment," video, MIT Sloan Center for Information Systems Research, 2005.

4. Even though comments in the annual report are carefully written and vetted, they do reveal important information about strategic direction that is useful beyond IT strategy. See, for example, Sarah Kaplan, Fiona Murray, and Rebecca Henderson, "Discontinuities in Senior Management: Assessing the Role of Recognition in Pharmaceutical Firm Response to Biotechnology," *Industrial and Corporate Change* 12, no. 2 (2003): 203–233.

5. Butch Leonardson interview, 2008.

6. See, for example, M. Porter, *Competitive Strategy: Techniques for Analyzing Industries and Competitors* (New York: Free Press, 1980), and

M. Porter, *Competitive Advantage: Creating and Sustaining Superior Performance* (New York: Free Press, 1985).

7. Sam Coursen interview conducted by Richard Hunter, July 29, 2008.

8. M. Smith and A. Apfel. "The Gartner Business Value Model: A Framework for Measuring Business Performance," Gartner Research Note G00139413, May 31, 2006.

9. Trey Lewis interview conducted by Richard Hunter, September 9, 2008.

Chapter 5

1. Interviews with Gonpo Tsering, COO, and Dieter Schlosser, CIO, DKSH, conducted by Richard Hunter, November 28, 2006, and November 15, 2006, respectively.

2. Richard Hunter and Dave Aron, "From Value to Advantage: Exploiting Information," Gartner Executive Programs Report, June 2004.

3. Guido Sacchi interview conducted by Richard Hunter, June 10, 2008.

4. Ken Venner interviews conducted by Richard Hunter, July 16, 2008, and November 20, 2006.

5. "2007 Award Recipient: Sharp HealthCare," Baldrige Committee, http://baldrige.nist.gov/PDF_files/Sharp_HealthCare_Profile.pdf.

6. Bill Spooner interviews conducted by Richard Hunter, November 17, 2006, and June 9, 2008.

7. Based on interviews with, and material from, the technology executive director of LFSCo, October 2006.

8. Interviews with Gonpo Tsering, COO, and Dieter Schlosser, CIO, DKSH, conducted by Richard Hunter, November 28, 2006, and November 15, 2006, respectively.

9. In our book *IT Risk: Turning Business Threats into Competitive Advantage* (Boston: Harvard Business School Publishing, 2007), we describe the importance of discussing trade-offs among four IT risks: availability, access, accuracy, and agility. We also show how rationalizing infrastructure and applications is the basis for reducing all four risks. Building short-term fixes in nonstandard ways can provide temporary agility, but it is not sustainable. Long-term resilience and agility depend on a well-structured and well-maintained foundation of infrastructure and applications. CIOs who can introduce risk trade-offs into their business discussions can often make the case for good decisions, such as adopting standardized practices, that otherwise could be difficult to justify based on schedules and financial returns.

Chapter 6

1. The value dials were developed by Sandra Morris and her IT team and have been published in multiple sources, including Jayne Mae and Robert A. Lansford, "It's the Metrics That Matter," *Intel Premier IT Professional*, Winter 2007, 16 (http://ipip.intel.com/go/99/its-the-metrics-that-matter/).

2. Most recently described in R. Hunter, A. Apfel, K. Mcgee, R. Handler, M. Smith, and W. Maurer, "A Simple Framework to Translate IT Benefits into Business Value Impact," Gartner Research Note G00156986, May 16, 2008.

3. "Motorola's Iridium Tab Is Higher Than Expected," July 14, 1999, http://www.thestreet.com/story/764251/1/motorolas-iridium-tab-is-higher-than-expected.html.

4. As described in F. Reichheld, *The Ultimate Question* (Harvard Business School Press, 2006), the net promoter score is the percentage of customers who respond with a score of 9–10 (out of 10) to the question, "How likely is it that you would you recommend [Company X] to a friend or colleague?" (also known as "promoters") minus the percentage of customers who score the same question 0–6 (also known as "detractors").

5. Randy Spratt interview conducted by Richard Hunter, December 7, 2006.

6. Karl Wachs interview conducted by George Westerman, Dallas TX, March 7, 2005. Included in Peter Weill, George Westerman, Chris Foglia, and Nils Fonstad, "Achieving Effective IT Oversight: Experienced CIOs Comment," video, MIT Sloan Center for Information Systems Research, 2005.

7. Sam Coursen interview conducted by Richard Hunter, July 29, 2008.

Chapter 7

1. R. Hunter, T. Nunno, and G. Waller, "Leading Enterprise Change," Gartner Executive Programs Signature Report, October 2005.

2. George Westerman and Peter Weill, "What Makes an Effective CIO: The Perspective of Non-IT Executives," *MIT Sloan CISR Research Briefings* V, 2C (July 2005).

3. Economist Intelligence Unit, "A Change for the Better: Steps for Successful Business Transformation," May 29, 2008.

4. Discussions with Gartner Executive Programs CIO members at workshops conducted at the organization's Forum meeting in Barcelona in spring 2005 showed that nearly 100 percent of attendees believed organizational

change could not be managed systematically. This result suggests that for many organizations, organizational change management is conceived in terms similar to those in which most organizations thought of project management in the 1970s and 1980s: as a "black art," a matter of leadership talent and luck more than methodology and skill, a fundamentally unmanageable endeavor whose results are unpredictable at best.

5. Standish Group, "The CHAOS Report (1994)," http://www.standishgroup.com/sample_research/chaos_1994_1.php.

6. E. Baldwin and M. Curley, *Managing IT Innovation for Business Value* (Santa Clara, CA: Intel Press, 2007).

7. M. Hammer, "Reengineering Work: Don't Automate, Obliterate," *Harvard Business Review* (July–August 1990): 104–112; M. Hammer and J. A. Champy, *Reengineering the Corporation: A Manifesto for Business Revolution* (New York: Harper Business Books, 1993); and T. H. Davenport, *Process Innovation: Reengineering Work Through Information Technology* (Boston: Harvard Business School Press, 1992).

8. Al-Noor Ramji interview conducted by George Westerman and Nils Fonstad, Cambridge, MA, March 15, 2005.

9. Risks of organizational change tend to have an uncomfortable profile for many companies. Although some people who are threatened by a change actively fight it, most people wait, heads down, and hope that the change will pass. Resistance disguises itself as apathy until it becomes apparent that the change is going to happen (such as when the application is coded and ready to be tested). Then argument, nitpicking, and sometimes even sabotage begin, sometimes bringing down even the best technically designed solutions. Managers who do not thoughtfully examine how the company really operates, and how an initiative will change that, open up risks not only to the project but also to their own careers.

10. As described in Gartner research by Kraft Bell and others, this form is similar to the seven stages of the grieving cycle described by Elisabeth Kübler-Ross. See R. Hunter, T. Nunno, and G. Waller, "Leading Enterprise Change," Gartner Executive Programs Signature Report, October 2005.

11. The three-lens framework, developed by faculty of behavioral policy and sciences at the MIT Sloan School of Management, was published in Deborah Ancona et al., *Managing for the Future: Organizational Behavior and Processes* (Cincinnati, OH: South-Western College Publishing, 2004). MIT Faculty—including Roberto Fernandez, Cyrus Gibson, and others—have used it effectively in teaching about organizational change for IT projects.

12. As described in Hunter, Nunno, and Waller, "Leading Enterprise Change."

13. George Westerman, Mark Cotteleer, Robert Austin, and Richard Nolan, "Tektronix, Inc: Global ERP Implementation," Case 9-699-043 (Boston: Harvard Business School, 1999).

14. Bud Mathaisel interview conducted by George Westerman and Peter Weill, Cambridge MA, May 19, 2005. Included in Peter Weill, George Westerman, Chris Foglia, and Nils Fonstad, "Achieving Effective IT Oversight: Experienced CIOs Comment," video, MIT Sloan Center for Information Systems Research, 2005.

15. For more on the importance of well-defined risk governance processes for the four A's, see George Westerman and Richard Hunter, *IT Risk: Turning Business Threats into Competitive Advantage* (Boston: Harvard Business School Publishing, 2007).

16. R. Hunter and M. Light, "Methodology and Productivity Study: The Analysis," Gartner Research Note SPA-480-1506, June 27, 1997.

17. The process is most effective in a risk-aware culture that encourages project teams to report risks promptly and accurately, as per our discussion of this topic in our book *IT Risk: Turning Business Threats into Competitive Advantage* (Boston: Harvard Business School Press, 2007).

18. Rebecca Rhoads, "RTN on Governance," presentation at MIT CISR summer session, Cambridge, Massachusetts, June 2005. Included in Peter Weill et al. video, "Achieving Effective IT Oversight."

Chapter 8

1. As cited in Dave Aron, Chuck Tucker, and Richard Hunter, "Show Me the Money: Advanced Practices in Benefits Realization," Gartner Executive Programs Signature Report, December 2005.

2. Among other problems with this mind-set is the fact that money is not the only scarce resource. Expertise in business processes and the systems that support them is often the scarcest resource in a fast-growing company where money is no object.

3. D. Flint, "The User's View of Why IT Projects Fail," Gartner Research Note G00124846, February 4, 2005.

4. John Hammergren interview conducted by Richard Hunter, December 6, 2006.

5. Anonymous CIO interview conducted by Richard Hunter, April 2008.

6. Richard Hunter and Tina Nunno, "Measuring the Value of Emerging Technologies," Report to Gartner Best Practices Council for Emerging Technologies Executives, September 25, 2006.

7. E. Brynjolfsson and L. Hitt, "Computing Productivity: Firm-Level Evidence," MIT Sloan School of Management Working Paper 4210-01, eBusiness@MIT Working Paper 139, June 2003.

8. Originally published in R. Hunter, T. Nunno, and R. Akerley, "Business Performance Is the Value of IT," Gartner Executive Programs CIO Signature report, April 2007.

9. Bob Wittstein interview conducted by Richard Hunter May 12, 2009. Note that layered governance mechanisms such as these are described in more detail in George Westerman and Richard Hunter, *IT Risk: Turning Business Threats into Competitive Advantage* (Boston: Harvard Business School Press, 2007).

Chapter 9

1. Randy Spratt interview conducted by Richard Hunter, July 25, 2008.

2. "CIO Values: Sam Coursen, VP and CIO, Freescale Semiconductor," *InformationWeek*, April 19, 2008, http://www.informationweek.com/news/management/interviews/showArticle.jhtml?articleID=207400183.

3. http://www.achievo.com/company/management_details.php?id=36; http://www.infoworld.com/d/adventures-in-it/2008-infoworld-cto-25-bud-mathaisel-achievo-721

4. http://www.infoworld.com/t/business/eds-buys-feld-group-in-89m-deal-077, http://public.cxo.com/conferences/speaker_detail.html?conferenceID=52&aid=12461&PHPSESSID=00845d8c7b23b3c99b7668a cdabfcd1b; http://www.evanta.com/details_popup.php?cmd=speaker&id=7287, http://www.cio.com/article/108900/Charles_Feld_on_Years_of_IT_Change, http://www.cio.com/article/101855/CIO_Hall_of_Fame_Charles_Feld

5. Randy Spratt interview, 2008.

6. Butch Leonardson interview conducted by Richard Hunter, June 10, 2008.

7. Net Promoter is a customer and employee loyalty program based on the research of Fred Reichheld, author of *Loyalty Rules: How Today's Leaders Build Lasting Relationships* (Boston: Harvard Business School Publishing, 2001), and *The Ultimate Question: Driving Good Profits and True Growth* (Boston: Harvard Business School Publishing, 2006).

8. http://www.achievo.com/company/management_details.php?id=36; http://www.infoworld.com/d/adventures-in-it/2008-infoworld-cto-25-bud-mathaisel-achievo-721; interview with Bud Mathaisel, Cambridge, MA, May 19, 2005, conducted by George Westerman and Peter Weill. Included in George Westerman, Peter Weill, Chris Foglia, and Nils Fonstad, "Building and Maintaining Credibility: Experienced CIOs Comment," video, MIT Sloan Center for Information Systems Research, 2005.

9. Guido Sacchi interview conducted by Richard Hunter, June 10, 2008.

10. Vignette compiled from public sources including http://www. businesswire.com/portal/site/google/?ndmViewId=news_view&newsId= 20071205006068&newsLang=en; http://content.members.fidelity.com/ Inside_Fidelity/fullStory/1,,7521,00.html; http://advice.cio.com/meridith_ levinson/marv_adams_has_left_citi_and_joined_fidelity.

INDEX

ABOUT THE AUTHORS

Richard Hunter is vice president and chief of research at Gartner Inc., where his recent work has focused on matters of interest to CIOs. He is the author of *World Without Secrets: Business, Crime and Privacy in the Age of Ubiquitous Computing* (Wiley, 2002) and coauthor (with George Westerman) of *IT Risk: Turning Business Threats into Competitive Advantage* (Harvard Business School Press, 2007).

Richard was elected a Gartner Fellow in 2003. He holds a bachelor's degree with a concentration in music from Harvard University. A world-class harmonica player, he is a leading composer of works for harmonica and the author of the world's best-selling method for jazz and rock harmonica players (*Jazz Harp*, Oak Publications, 1980).

George Westerman is a research scientist in the Center for Information Systems Research (CISR) at MIT's Sloan School of Management, and faculty chair for the course IT for the Non-IT Executive. His research and teaching examine management challenges at the interface between CIOs and business executives.

George is coauthor (with Richard Hunter) of *IT Risk: Turning Business Threats into Competitive Advantage*, which *CIO Insight* magazine named one of its Best Books of 2007. His research has been published in management journals such as *Sloan Management Review, IESE Insight,* and *Organization Science* as well as numerous case studies, book chapters, and industry publications.

Prior to earning his doctorate at Harvard Business School, George gained more than a dozen years of IT and management experience. He is a noted speaker and workshop facilitator with IT and non-IT executives, and a member of several nonprofit boards.